TALENT TRANSFORMATION

TALENT
TRANSFORMATION

Develop Today's
Team for Tomorrow's
World of Work

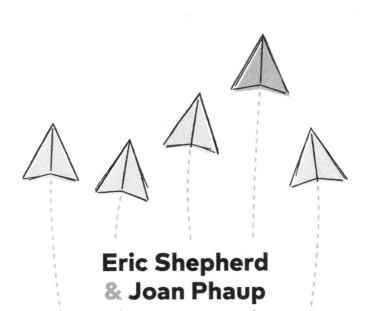

**Eric Shepherd
& Joan Phaup**

ISBN 978-1-7355851-0-9 (paperback)
ISBN 978-1-7355851-2-3 (ebook)

Published by Talent Transformation Press
www.talenttransformation.com

Produced by Page Two
www.pagetwo.com

www.talenttransformation.com/book

CONTENTS

ACKNOWLEDGMENTS

W E COULD NOT have written this book without the support of our family, friends, colleagues, advisors, cheerleaders, and previewers.

We would like to take this opportunity to thank all the people who have been there for us during our journeys in life—those who have counseled, motivated, taught, corrected, influenced, and encouraged us to be our best selves. Without your help this book would not have been possible.

To list everyone we appreciate would take an encyclopedia. Please know that we are grateful to you all.

Special thanks to those whose sound guidance and constructive advice have kept us on track:

Graham Phaup, Supportive
  and Patient Husband
Laura Bonazzoli,
  Development Editor
Martin Belton, Advisor
  and Previewer
Elliott Masie, Inspirer
Mike Cooke, Inspirer
Mike Pino, Previewer
  and Inspirer

Bill Coscarelli, Previewer
G Harris, Previewer
Gene Hawkins, Previewer
James Lehman, Previewer
James Lower, Previewer
Jim Parry, Previewer
John Horton, Previewer
John Kleeman, Previewer
Judith Hale, Previewer
Logan Block, Previewer

PREFACE

WITH THE MANY models we have for evaluating talent, employee performance, and management solutions, you might wonder if we need another.

But the Fourth Industrial Revolution is bringing to the workplace dramatic changes that call for a comprehensive approach to talent transformation—a framework for helping C-suite executives, HR leaders, and coaches improve current performance and prepare the workforce for the new jobs and careers that will emerge in the coming years.

The Talent Transformation Pyramid (p. 47) addresses this need. The pyramid offers a shared vocabulary for discussing the factors that support competencies—everything from personality traits, emotional intelligence, and psychological safety to functional and cognitive skills. It also provides a means of evaluating individuals and teams broadly and deeply to assess their current performance, identify appropriate interventions, and determine readiness for ever-changing job roles.

We bring to this writing our combined four decades of experience in the talent, learning, and assessment management fields, paired with service on boards and continuous conversations with executives, HR leaders, coaches, and consultants.

As CEO of a multinational assessment software company for eighteen years, Eric Shepherd wholeheartedly championed the need for trustable workplace assessments, from surveys and diagnostic tools to compliance tests and certification exams. After stepping down from that role, he explored psychological assessments and new means of collecting data about on-the-job performance.

Seeking a deeper understanding of the factors that support the competence of individuals, teams, and organizations, Eric studied psychology, Artificial Intelligence (AI), and coaching. He interviewed leaders, practitioners, and academics from all over the world to discover how they are currently deploying new technologies and how organizations plan to change for the new world of work.

Attempting to model the insights he'd gained, Eric experimented with Venn diagrams, flow charts, enterprise modeling, and other visuals until a pyramid of triangles within triangles finally struck home. After several iterations, the Talent Transformation Pyramid emerged as a practical model for discussing and measuring the factors that support competencies and strengthen organizational performance.

Leaders, managers, and coaches from small regional companies to large multinational organizations use the pyramid's vocabulary to tease out what's required to support the behaviors required on the job. The pyramid helps promote understanding regarding the difference between behaviors and capabilities and their supporting factors.

When Eric decided it was time to write a book explaining the pyramid, he turned to his colleague Joan Phaup. The two quickly resumed the roles they'd established when they began working together in the nineties. Eric drafted chapter outlines, then shared his findings and concepts with Joan, often drawing diagrams as he spoke. Joan brought these elements together, put them into words, and posed questions for clarification.

Our greatest challenge has been to keep pace with a world that is changing beneath our feet. We set out on our journey in the summer of 2019 anticipating massive changes in the workplace, but we had no idea that a pandemic would accelerate them. We hope this book, which builds on the work of the many researchers and writers who came before us, inspires readers to prepare for and embrace the profound changes that will follow it.

INTRODUCTION

POWERFUL TECHNOLOGIES and new business models are remaking the workplace, setting the stage for new jobs and careers, and empowering individuals and teams to advance organizational goals through creativity and collaboration. The Fourth Industrial Revolution presents enormous challenges and opportunities at high speed, calling on leaders to move quickly and plan for a dramatically different world of work.

How will competency models, assessments, and learning keep pace with this revolution? Our current practices have worked by helping us recognize the challenges and opportunities of the twentieth century and develop skills to address them. But new ways of work demand new solutions that embrace changes in technology, social attitudes, and business models. As we witnessed at the onset of COVID-19, agility and flexibility enabled many people to adopt new practices with surprising speed. These qualities will help them navigate the coming years of exponential change.

The Talent Transformation Pyramid (p. 47) addresses the questions that leaders, managers, and coaches face today:

- How can we promote a culture in which people enjoy their roles and perform well within a continually changing workplace?

- How will we evaluate competencies and identify the factors that support them?

- How can we use data to evaluate culture fit and job fit?

- How can we gauge someone's potential for taking on new responsibilities and performing well?

- How can we help individuals adapt to using new technologies to perform in new or updated roles?

About This Book

Talent Transformation answers these questions with a strategic approach for improving performance. The Talent Transformation Pyramid brings together twelve factors that enable the success of individuals, teams, and entire organizations. These factors include technical and functional skills as well as the social, emotional, and conversational intelligences that enable robust, meaningful relationships. This framework also acknowledges that psychological safety, a supportive culture, free-flowing information, and appropriate tools are crucial to performance. The creation of workplaces that empower teams of people with diverse skills and backgrounds is critical for success in the twenty-first century.

Understanding the twelve factors, measuring them accurately, and finding correlations among them will guide you in determining interventions that will help your workforce build competencies for current and future jobs. This approach is viable thanks to new technologies that make it possible to collect vast amounts of data, identify patterns, correlate findings, and determine causation.

In writing this book, we have tapped into the wisdom and experience of the researchers, thinkers, and practitioners whose work has brought measurement, assessment, and talent management to the point where organizations can address the challenges and opportunities ahead. We have also built on our affiliation with the Talent Transformation Guild—a community of executives, human resource leaders, talent development specialists, personal coaches, and consultants who want to keep pace with the technology-driven revolution now underway.

Who Should Read It?

We have designed this book to help executives, leaders, managers, and human resources professionals create a better work environment today while meeting tomorrow's demands. We assume that you as a reader

- want to create a harmonious, high-performing team or coach others to do so;

- see dramatic changes looming in the workplace and wish to prepare for them;

- know about factors that affect performance but would like to understand better how these factors interact to support success; and

- welcome fresh approaches to talent transformation.

How to Use It

We recommend reading this book straight through, but since each chapter stands on its own, you can skip around as much as you wish. If you are an expert in the subject of a particular chapter or feel out of your depth, feel free to skip ahead. We hope you will keep the book for reference when you encounter issues and need to refresh your understanding. The nine chapters in this book will give you plenty to do:

1. Explore the Fourth Industrial Revolution's impact on how tasks will change as powerful technologies generate massive job losses and gains. Recognize the urgent need to prepare for these changes through reskilling.

2. Get pointers for managing change, reassigning tasks to take advantage of helpful technologies, and positioning workers to learn new competencies or succeed in their roles.

3. Meet the Talent Transformation Pyramid—the heart of this book and our inspiration for writing it! Here, we describe twelve factors that underpin individual, team, and organizational success, from behaviors and work environments to technical and functional skills. We explain the importance of measuring the factors individually and correlating the results to help you determine valuable interventions for building competence.

4. Trace the progress of assessment as an increasingly reliable means of measuring personalities and functional skills. Read about the many uses of assessments and get a glimpse of how they may change in an age of massive-scale automation.

5. Delve into the science of measurement and the principles that support valid, reliable assessment. Get pointers on mitigating potential errors of measurement, defending against fraud, and understanding assessment results.

6. Find out how assessments based on clearly defined competencies can help predict how well and how safely individuals are likely to perform the tasks their roles require. Discover options for assessment delivery, including innovative approaches to predicting job readiness.

7. Discover how teams benefit from personality, strength-finder, and emotional intelligence assessments, which can inform team selection and help members of new teams understand themselves and each other. Assessments can also help established teams regain their sense of direction when problems emerge.

8. Investigate how to improve organizational results and decision-making by tracking metrics and detecting correlations. This chapter discusses the importance of identifying sound goals and

monitoring progress using Key Performance Indicators (KPIs), Objectives and Key Results (OKRs), and other methods.

9. Consider the impacts of four trends that are changing the way we live and learn: blended technologies, innovative business models, a growing emphasis on social responsibility, and new ways to nurture and inspire talent. Consider how the Talent Transformation Pyramid, by providing a strategic approach to defining competencies and the factors for successful performance, could help you engage and energize your workforce.

Where to Learn More

Visit the Talent Transformation Guild at www.talenttransformation .com/book for information that supplements this book and for access to white papers, webcasts, podcasts, videos, and more. You are welcome to contact us at book@talenttransformation.com to discuss any aspect of this book. We're keen to learn too!

We hope this book makes work more enjoyable, engaging, and fulfilling for you, your colleagues, and your clients.

THE TRANSFORMING
WORKPLACE

THE RISE OF new technologies had already brought sweeping changes to the world of work when a worldwide emergency, the COVID-19 pandemic, accelerated this transformation.

The technologies were ready for this crisis, enabling the rapid, widespread adoption of telemedicine, teleworking, food delivery, and other responses to this global emergency. Practically overnight, people embraced these innovations as necessities of life. Like many others, we had been expecting significant changes in the world of work in the coming years, but the speed with which millions of people jumped online and began working from home took us by surprise.

The coronavirus wave has injected increased energy into the digital transformation of daily life and work. When that wave recedes, technologies that support new working practices such as video-conferencing, Machine Learning (ML), Artificial Intelligence (AI), autonomous robots, and robotic processes will continue to drive significant changes across many industries. These technologies are challenging organizations to rethink their strategic plans, redesign their processes and work environments, and retrain their workers.

No one knows what the future will look like, but it's likely to bring continuing uncertainty in terms of job security, availability, and requirements. As the world recovers from the pandemic and adopts new technologies, some fear a second tsunami of unemployment and its accompanying economic and social stressors. Others welcome technological innovation, predicting a future in which machines will increasingly perform our most basic and tedious tasks, enabling humans to work with greater creativity and fulfillment.

Whichever vision you hold, we can agree that studying the changes already underway can help prepare us for the more dramatic developments to come. In short, now is the time to recognize the challenges of change, glimpse new possibilities, and start planning for what's ahead. This book can help by providing a framework for understanding competencies, assessment, and measurement that will support leaders, managers, and workers in this new world of work.

In this chapter, we quickly review the history that has led us to this point. Then we discuss how automation is changing the workplace, describe the essential skills workers will need, and explore how training and education can help workers acquire these skills. We also note some organizations whose pioneering efforts are helping to upgrade the workforce.

A Brief History of Workplace Change

Workplace change is perpetual and inevitable and is often enabled by new discoveries, inventions, and social attitudes. In each of the three major transitions that preceded our present-day transformation, new jobs replaced outdated ones. In response, people migrated, joined new communities, and adopted new ways of living.

Water and Steam Mechanization

The First Industrial Revolution began around 1765, as water and steam mechanization began to transform an agrarian economy to an industrial one. The increased production of textiles brought farmhands from the countryside into cities and towns and gave everyone more types of clothing to choose from. Extensive coal mining and the advent of the steam-powered locomotive expanded railroads, making it easier to move goods over long distances and build more widespread trade.

Electricity and Mass Production

In the late nineteenth century, the ability to generate and distribute electricity enabled mass production and led to the expansion of virtually all industries. Public power replaced candles and gas lamps for lighting homes, factories, and city streets. During the Second Industrial Revolution, we swapped horses and buggies for streetcars and automobiles. We communicated by telegraph, then by telephone. We tuned into news and entertainment on radio, then on television. We jumped into our cars to drive on superhighways, then we went farther and faster by air.

Information Technology

The rise of electronics, telecommunications, and computers and Information Technology (IT) sped us up even more. At first, IT simply streamlined data entry and retrieval, but the Third Industrial Revolution soon brought us the Internet and the World Wide Web. Smartphones and other mobile devices freed us to access information anytime, anywhere.

Exponential Change

Now we have entered a period of more dramatic change. The World Economic Forum (WEF) calls this Fourth Industrial Revolution "a new chapter in human development, enabled by extraordinary technology advances commensurate with those of the First, Second, and Third Industrial Revolutions. These advances are merging the physical, digital, and biological worlds in ways that create both huge promise and potential peril."

We are now seeing unprecedented transformations in production, management, and governance systems. Automation technologies are taking on many tasks that people have done until now. Machine-generated algorithms have made voice, facial, and intricate pattern recognition commonplace. These algorithms have plenty of data to use, thanks to powerful handheld devices, cloud computing, and the Internet of Things (IoT)—the interconnection of computing devices embedded in everyday objects, which enables security systems, thermostats, electronic appliances, lights, and many other items to send and receive data.

The COVID-19 Pandemic

We might regard today's burgeoning technologies as enablers of change and the COVID-19 pandemic as an accelerator of change. Self-isolation—suggested or imposed by governments—meant that millions of people would work from home or stop working altogether. Some of those who could only perform their tasks at a specific location started learning new skills online to brighten their career opportunities. Employees rapidly learned to perform a variety of tasks at home that they had previously completed in the workplace. Having been forced to embrace teleworking, many people and their employers now know its benefits. Remote work does not suit everyone, but it's become a popular alternative to commuting.

International collaboration enabled by technology accelerated the understanding of pathogen transmission and helped improve infection testing, vaccination trials, and drug development. The combination of AI, ML, cloud computing, and biotechnologies empowered scientists, healthcare workers, and citizens to prepare for and cope with the pandemic. A single technology could not have provided the insights required, but a combination of technologies made it possible to address some problems in days or weeks that might otherwise have taken years to solve.

How Technology Is Transforming Work

Technological progress will impact all aspects of life, but it may be that employers and workers feel its implications most acutely.

The Future of Work in America, a 2019 report from the McKinsey Global Institute, observed:

> Technology is altering the day-to-day mix of activities associated with more and more jobs over time. The occupational mix of the economy is changing, and the demand for skills is changing along with it. Employers will need to manage large-scale workforce transformations that could involve redefining business processes and workforce needs, retraining and moving some people into new roles, and creating programs for continuous learning. These transformations could present opportunities to upgrade jobs and make them more rewarding.

Indeed, people taking on new roles will need to prepare for them by cultivating not only their technical skills but also their creativity, flexibility, and ability to engage, cooperate, and collaborate.

This book mentions a variety of technologies. You can learn more about them in Appendix A: Glossary of Technologies (p. 211).

Given that technology is growing exponentially, we also are maintaining an up-to-date list online, one of many additional resources you will find on our website at www.talenttransformation.com/book.

Job Loss and Creation

Although modernized technologies have always caused outmoded jobs to disappear, they have also created new ones. A few decades ago, word processors quickly made secretarial pools obsolete. However, with the proper training, stenographers and typists adapted to the use of the latest technologies. There turned out to be plenty of work for other people too since computer hardware needed repairing and software required programming. Eventually, the Internet created jobs in network engineering.

Today, we can expect even more dramatic changes in employment, as explained in *The Future of Jobs Report 2018* by the WEF:

> Disruptive changes to business models will have a profound impact on the employment landscape over the coming years. Many of the major drivers of transformation currently affecting global industries are expected to have a significant impact on jobs, ranging from significant job creation to job displacement, and from heightened labor productivity to widening skills gaps. In many industries and countries, the most in-demand occupations or specialties did not exist ten or even five years ago, and the pace of change is set to accelerate.

How is this job loss and creation likely to occur? Robots and automation are taking on many dull, repetitive, demeaning, and dangerous tasks, as well as those that require physical endurance or precise movement. The new tasks that will emerge for people are expected to require more typically human skills, such as creativity, communication, and empathy.

In the past, marketing assistants with basic administrative skills could serve their employers well. But Robotic Process Automation (RPA) that responds to prospects and chatbots that reduce the need for customized correspondence have replaced many administrative tasks. These days, marketing assistants might help configure RPA and chatbots. Their jobs remain, but some of their tasks are new and call for more creativity and critical thinking, not to mention the ability to use more sophisticated technologies than they did before.

Retail staff equipped with mobile point-of-sale devices are free to move around a store to interact with customers. Spending less time at the cash register and more time engaging with people calls for empathy, patience, and the ability to build trust with customers, plus a greater awareness of which products might meet the customers' needs. What might have been a routine job will be more interesting, but also more demanding.

Increased Demand for Higher Technical Skills

As automation takes on more low-skilled tasks, people will need new skills for handling more creative and technical tasks. As an example, the advent of big data, online analytical processing, and ML brings with it the need for more highly skilled technicians to configure and maintain these technologies.

Factories are deploying robots, AI, IoT, RPA, cloud computing, cognitive computing, and Cyber-Physical Systems (CPS) that control or monitor mechanisms with computer-based algorithms. To interact with such swiftly changing technologies, the people who work in such factories need to enhance their technical knowledge and skills. Everyone from robot technicians and machinists to automation engineers and interface developers will need to up their game.

Many other sectors of the economy—notably technology, healthcare, and energy—are undergoing massive technology-driven change and will need workers to keep pace with it.

Increased Demand for Social and Communication Skills

It may seem surprising, but workers in this technology-driven age will need high levels of the interpersonal skills that enable people to work effectively together.

As Deloitte, a multinational professional services network, notes in "The Future of Work in Manufacturing":

> The rise of automation in the workplace has brought with it an interesting corollary for skills needed in human workers. As technology replaces many of the manual or repetitive tasks many jobs entail, it frees up space for skills that are uniquely human, often called "soft" skills... As digital transformation and the Fourth Industrial Revolution continue to redefine manufacturing jobs of the future, leaders and workers alike need to embrace a work environment that is expected to blend advanced technology and digital skills with uniquely human skills, to yield the highest level of productivity.

Working successfully in a complex environment involving complicated processes and multiple technologies will require effective teamwork and collaboration. Employers will look for adaptability, creativity, and emotional intelligence—the ability to be aware of, control, and express one's emotions; empathize with other people; and sensitively handle interpersonal relationships.

As Deloitte's "From Jobs to Superjobs: 2019 Global Human Capital Trends" noted:

> The jobs of today are more machine-powered and data-driven than in the past, and they also require more human skills in problem-solving, communication, interpretation, and design. As machines replace humans in doing routine work, jobs are evolving that require new combinations of human skills and capabilities. This creates the need for organizations to redesign jobs—along with their business and work processes—to keep pace.

To redesign a job after a machine takes over some aspects of it, you will need to clarify the remaining tasks to be performed and the competencies they require, then update related competency models, job descriptions, training materials, and assessments.

See Chapter 6 for a more detailed discussion of competency models. Chapter 9 suggests how competencies and credentials will likely evolve.

Based on conversations with leaders and research of job needs, we regard the following ten skills as essential for successful adaptation to the new employment landscape:

1. **Complex Problem-solving:** New challenges call for the ability to solve novel, complex, ill-defined problems that organizations have never encountered before.

2. **Critical Thinking:** Analyzing facts to form a judgment requires healthy skepticism, rational thought, and unbiased evaluation of the evidence.

3. **Creativity:** Previous patterns of success will not always apply, so workers will need imagination and original ideas to form new business models, solutions, and processes.

4. **People Management:** For people to engage passionately with their work, they need to be treated as complex individuals with social and emotional needs.

5. **Coordinating with Others:** Teams must coordinate creatively and multilaterally to design, deploy, and maintain complex systems and machines.

6. **Social, Conversational, and Emotional Intelligence:** Handling interpersonal relationships respectfully is essential as people with diverse skillsets come together to solve challenges.

7. **Decision-making:** The ability to rapidly understand the facts related to a given problem and recognize the benefits and risks of each potential solution enables workers to form sound judgments and make timely decisions.

8. **Service Orientation:** As automation increasingly performs logical, repetitive tasks, and as product distinctions narrow, each organization will be distinguished from others by its employees' abilities to service customers' needs.

9. **Negotiation:** Those who can manage conversations amid change, competition, and complexity will be able to reach agreements that benefit both sides and result in synergistic relationships.

10. **Cognitive Flexibility:** The ability to think deeply about complicated scenarios, switching rapidly from one to another, engenders creative new ways of working.

Emergence of Talent Marketplaces

Digital platforms that connect freelancers with organizations that need them are transforming the way many people find work. These digital marketplaces can identify people to add capacity or source individuals with specialized skills for specific projects. Examples of such skills include data entry, graphic design, website construction, software development, data analytics, legal review, writing, and instructional design. Taking on tasks on a moment's notice, freelancers can start or reinvigorate projects that have been languishing. Contracts can be set up on an hourly or per-project basis.

Independent contractors and freelancers have long been part of the economy, but these new talent marketplaces have made it far easier to match supply with demand. Back-to-back agreements between employers and gig workers make it easy to contract for required services on a short-term basis, such as lining up rideshare drivers, or on a longer-term basis, such as hiring engineers to maintain websites. Talent marketplaces can quickly match available work with freelancers who have the skills required. As with any marketplace, these platforms also influence the rate of pay, increasing it for in-demand skills and decreasing it for less sought-after skills.

Although talent marketplaces provide tremendous job flexibility and autonomy, they deprive independent workers of the benefits—including sick leave, paid vacation, health insurance, and retirement plans—that permanent employees earn. Like permanent employees, gig workers need to keep their skills up to date; to do this, they must pay for their own training and certifications.

Reskilling the Automated Workplace

Digital transformation—the use of new, fast, and frequently changing digital technology to solve problems—creates new kinds of jobs that require specialized skills. During previous phases of industry, employees could expect to graduate from school or college, join an employer, and stay there for many years. But today's workers tend to change roles and organizations more often. Employees are starting a job, learning how to do it, then taking on new and different tasks and roles. From what we have seen to date, we expect to see a pattern of learn/work/change—and repeat, with people less likely to stay in the same job for a long time.

Reskilling—preparing workers for these new roles—is likely to become a fundamental responsibility of most organizations. To support reskilling, organizations will need to assess workers' existing skills accurately, then provide training that builds on their potential to contribute more to the organization. Successful reskilling will enable organizations to empower their workers to take on roles that require more knowledge and expertise and are potentially more satisfying. Upskilling, on the other hand, will help employees who stay in their current position (or a similar role) to use the tools of the digital workplace. In this book, we will sometimes use the term "reskilling" generically, embracing the idea of upgrading skills for any worker, whether they are moving to a higher level or staying in their current role.

Benefits and Costs of Reskilling

Improving existing workers' skills, knowledge, and behaviors will save employers from having to recruit new talent while giving them a more productive workforce. In turn, workers will gain better job prospects. But at what cost?

The WEF 2019 report, *Towards a Reskilling Revolution: Industry-Led Action for the Future of Work*, noted limited availability of information about the business case and return on investment of reskilling. The recent upheaval brought on by the COVID-19 pandemic has produced even more wild cards. But in looking toward the coming decade, the report estimated the cost of reskilling displaced workers in the United States during the 2020s at about $34 billion. These costs would include wages, lost productivity, and benefits while a worker spends time learning. The report indicated that, in the United States alone, companies could reskill 25 percent of workers in disrupted jobs. The report suggested that companies could work with each other to reduce reskilling costs. Also, governments and taxpayers could take on some of the cost as a societal investment, and the private and public sectors could collaborate to achieve economies of scale.

The Role of Education in Reskilling

Institutions of higher education around the world are adapting to new demands by training skilled researchers, engineers, and computer scientists. However, the K–12 educational pipeline feeding these institutions still focuses to a great extent on teaching skills valued in the nineteenth and twentieth centuries. Too many schools are training young people for a world of traditional factories and centralized decision-making. In misguided efforts to improve student outcomes, they're investing their resources on programs designed for a previous era, when they should be anticipating what's ahead.

Skill shortages today are, in part, a result of not developing the right curricula in years past. Thankfully, there are many initiatives around the world partnering industry and education to resolve this. Everyone from politicians to departments of education to school administrators, teachers, and parents will need to support learning environments that cultivate the behaviors and capabilities of workers for the next era.

Exemplars of Reskilling

As organizations gain a better understanding of the skills required, many are launching ambitious training initiatives. Here are some examples:

- The Grow with Google program—provided by Google in partnership with libraries, schools, and nonprofits—offers people in the United States and Canada free training so they can pick up skills needed to compete in the digital age.

- The professional services firm PricewaterhouseCoopers announced in 2019 that it would be investing $3 billion over the next three to four years in upskilling.

- In 2019, Amazon committed to investing $700 million to upskill 100,000 employees by 2025.

- Accenture's "Job Buddy" software allows employees to examine what their skills are, what areas of their work are likely to be automated, and what training will help.

- In 2019, IBM chose soft skills to focus on in five new professional training modules: Collaborate Effectively, Presenting with Purpose, Interpersonal Skills, Delivering Quality Work with Agility, and Solving Problems with Critical and Creative Thinking.

- Walmart Academy retrained 720,000 employees in advanced retail skills, leadership, and change management over two years.

- The WEF's Closing the Skills Gap 2020 coalition has secured pledges for reskilling or upskilling more than 17 million people globally. The initiative uses a virtual hub to capture measurable commitments from leading companies to train, reskill, and upskill workers. The hub also serves as a repository of best practices and case studies.

- L'Oréal has helped 1,000 executives develop digital roadmaps for their offices and regions to encourage openness, innovation, and agility.

- Lloyds Banking Group has planned for 4.4 million hours of learning to help employees handle agile project management and AI.

A sense of promise and opportunity pervades these efforts, which focus not just on the need to mitigate the challenges presented by technological change, but also to embrace the possibilities it offers.

Takeaways

- Throughout history, new technologies have disrupted the workplace.

- The Fourth Industrial Revolution will change the nature of work, bring job losses and job gains, increase demand for both highly technical and interpersonal skills, and promote the emergence of talent marketplaces.

- Machine-powered, data-driven jobs require more human skills in problem-solving, communication, interpretation, and design.

- The reshaping of work calls for reskilling the workforce through on-the-job training and formal education.

EMBRACING
CHANGE

THE ANCIENT GREEK philosopher Heraclitus observed that change is the only constant in life. The motto is famous to this day, and as we saw in the last chapter, it certainly applies to the workplace. However, unlike previous transitional periods, this century is bringing change at breakneck speed.

In his 2001 essay "The Law of Accelerating Returns," futurist Ray Kurzweil predicted profound technological advances: "An analysis of the history of technology shows that technological change is exponential, contrary to the common-sense 'intuitive linear' view. So we won't experience one hundred years of progress in the twenty-first century—it will be more like 20,000 years of progress (at today's rate)."

World Economic Forum (WEF) Founder and Executive Chairman Klaus Schwab wrote in 2015 that "like the revolutions that preceded it, the Fourth Industrial Revolution has the potential to raise global income levels and improve the quality of life for populations around the world." Schwab also noted the potential for long-term gains in efficiency and productivity as well as some serious challenges, notably greater inequality between low-skill, low-pay jobs and high-skill, high-pay jobs. Schwab commented that "the changes are so profound that, from the perspective of human history, there has never been a time of greater promise or potential peril."

Whatever their ups and downs, organizations can embrace change as the new norm and manage it proactively. Jobs are already morphing, emerging, and receding within the span of a few years. As society accepts one level of change, new situations arise, new automation activates, and another level of change occurs. We witnessed this with the COVID-19 outbreak, which quickly converted people into remote workers, many of whom now regard working from home as a sensible alternative to commuting.

The future offers tremendous opportunities to organizations that adopt new technologies and use them effectively. Preparing for the next wave of progress calls for a clear vision for the future, deliberate planning, and effective communication with the workforce.

Visualize, Plan, and Communicate Your Transformation Strategy

We extol visionary leaders, from Winston Churchill to Steve Jobs. But these leaders could not have realized their visions without a roadmap for change and the ability to communicate in ways that inspired others to join them. Here are four essential steps that lay the groundwork for successful change.

Develop a Clear Vision for Change

Developing a clear vision is the first step in any change effort. Why? A clear vision sets expectations and guides the planning that is essential for effective execution.

A compelling vision for automation and talent transformation will answer the question: "Where do we want to be?" Briefly describing an organization's future desired or ideal state helps individuals understand its vision and align their actions with it.

To develop a clear vision, consider these types of questions:

1. How do we want to transform our organization using automation and technology?

2. Why is digital and talent transformation core to organizational success?

3. What will the organization look and feel like after transformation?

4. How can our organization navigate transformation successfully?

Once the brainstorming has teased out answers to these questions, you're ready to communicate your vision in ways that empower and guide the stakeholders. Typically, the vision will do one or more of the following:

1. Describe an ideal state with words such as: "Our workforce and automation will be learning from each other to improve customer satisfaction."

2. Describe an ideal perception, such as: "Employees enjoy partnering with automation to get things done effectively and efficiently."

3. Reference an organization with words like: "Delivering higher levels of satisfaction than our competitors at less cost."

Define Objectives

In contrast to the vision statement, objectives briefly describe the steps required to achieve the transformation and realize the vision.

During the early stages of planning for change, you might lean toward developing comprehensive roadmaps; however, this is unnecessary and can even be counterproductive. Employee buy-in is essential at this stage, and brief objectives can help guide them in proposing steps for achieving the vision rather than prescribing or dictating required actions.

Develop your objectives using a similar process to the one you used to create the vision; explore the following topics that will help leaders tease out ideas for realizing the vision:

- Requirements to achieve the vision
- A sequence of activities required to achieve the vision promptly, without unnecessarily impacting clients or employees
- High-level tasks and processes to be automated
- How employees will benefit from the transformation
- How employees will be trained, at a high level, to cope with the changes and perform the new tasks
- How to communicate the vision and objectives to employees
- How to communicate the vision and objectives to clients
- Which role or team is responsible for successful transformation
- Which role or team is responsible for automation governance

After addressing these issues, you should be ready to develop your objectives.

Communicate Transparently

With a clear vision and objectives in place, you can start to communicate with the broader organization.

Organizational change can trigger negativity and resistance. Employees might feel threatened by or even fearful of automation, new devices, cloud computing, and the Internet of Things (IoT). These concerns and fears deserve attention. If left unaddressed, they will undermine your transformation strategies.

It is essential to communicate your vision for the impending change. Employees who do not understand the vision may become paralyzed by imagining worst-case scenarios or refuse to help change the current system at any cost. Others may misunderstand the pace of the change effort and want to push forward without proper planning. Either of these responses can derail change efforts. So, it's important to clearly explain why the change is imperative, describe the drawbacks of the current situation, note the need for a systematic approach, and mention how you expect the change to make things better. These benefits could include

- the assignment of repetitive, dull, or unhealthy tasks to machines;

- the creation of new, more intriguing, and satisfying jobs drawing on a broader range of workers' talents; and/or

- improvement in the quality of products and services.

Transparent communication keeps everyone in the organization up to date on the change activities underway. Providing regular notifications explaining each aspect of the change prevents people from making assumptions—often negative ones. Sincere, open communication can reassure employees who have justifiable concerns related to their jobs, tasks, and the organization's future. Here are some pointers for clear communications:

- Expose all the facts—pros and cons—so people feel they can trust what you are saying.

- Remind people that the changes underway are crucial and explain why.

- Communicate frequently, perhaps even by way of daily briefings.

- Provide diagrams to help people picture the past, present, and future.

- Use various mediums, from podcasts and videocasts to emails, phone calls, and in-person presentations.

Depending on the organization and its digital transformation strategy, your communications might address questions such as these:

- Why are we introducing automation?

- How will automation help our organization grow?

- Why is our current process/model/state unsustainable?

- How will we implement the change?

- How does the change reflect our organization's mission, vision, and values?

- How will the change benefit employees, and what part can they play in the process?

- What are our commitments toward the people the change will affect?

- Who can answer employees' questions regarding the change, and how should employees contact them?

- How will management keep everyone abreast of progress?

Overcome Resistance

The resistance of some employees to a move they regard as uninspired or divorced from organizational values could cascade into negativity and slow down the change process. Nurturing a positive organizational culture and healthy relationships among colleagues can decrease this resistance. Understanding how people might respond to change is a good starting point. Here are four typical responses to change:

1. "Critics" oppose the change.

2. "Victims" fear the change.

3. The "disinterested" ignore the change.

4. "Navigators" drive the change and involve others in making it successful.

An organization must convert all types of responders into navigators. Here are some ways to make that happen:

- Explain the dangers of not changing.

- Eliminate uncertainty as much as possible.

- Invite everyone's ideas and opinions before making a decision.
- Reiterate the reasons behind the change whenever possible.
- Reward and recognize any positive steps toward the objectives.
- Keep communication as transparent as possible.

Resolve the Struggle between Opposing Forces

People often embrace change right away, but in many cases, moving past the status quo and overcoming resistance calls for extra effort. Psychologist Kurt Lewin's concept of force field analysis is a strategic tool that can clarify the prerequisites for a successful change. According to Lewin, change incubates a struggle between driving forces that want to push the reform forward and restraining forces that wish to resist it. Lewin noted that inside an organization, there will always be forces on either side of the equation. When both forces are equivalent in power, change is impossible.

Examples of driving forces include a desire to grow, a desire to win, market changes, increased use of new technology, competitive threats, regulatory reform, stakeholder opinions, and incentives. Restraining forces might include resistance by the individuals who want to maintain the status quo due to a fear of failure, current inertia, apathy, or even hostility.

Change is possible when the driving factors collectively outweigh the restraining factors. As we have witnessed during the pandemic, the dominant driving force of protecting public health helped overcome resistance to new working practices.

Disrupt the Equilibrium

Before the introduction of a change, forces that maintain the status quo are in play. Making change requires disrupting this equilibrium. Leaders have two choices here: Strengthen the driving forces by introducing favorable conditions or eliminate conditions that empower the restraining forces. Again, whenever the driving forces exceed the restraining forces, change is possible.

Lewin's analysis enables us to understand the emotions that lead a person to embrace or resist a change. In most situations, there will be people on both sides of the equation. Individuals who are unhappy and resistant to change may well be moving through various emotional states, as Elisabeth Kübler-Ross describes in her model of the grief response (Figure 2.1):

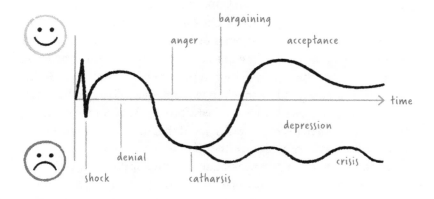

Figure 2.1: Elisabeth Kübler-Ross's Five Stages of Grief

Analyzing and understanding the reasons behind people's resistance reveals ways to make the change more comfortable and acceptable. To understand emotions that trigger resistance to change, you would need to engage in dialogue with the individual to understand their personality and past experiences of change and what they recognize as its risks. You would also need to explain the planned mitigations and the benefits of success. These steps will dampen the effects of emotions that might trigger resistance.

Use Force Field Analysis
Not all forces are related to human behaviors, but to use this analysis, we need to understand what influences ourselves and others.

Emotional intelligence enables us to do that. Learning to be self-aware and tuned in to others' emotions makes it easier to identify behaviors related to driving and restraining forces. Here are some steps for using force field analysis effectively:

1. Clearly document your vision regarding the change; define in detail the status quo and the desired state.

2. Identify the driving forces and restraining forces and record them on a force field diagram (Figure 2.2).

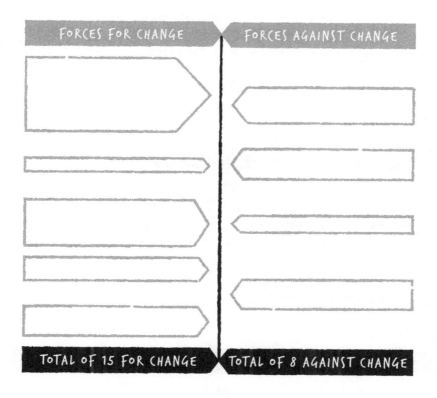

Figure 2.2: Kurt Lewin's Force Field Analysis

3. Evaluate the impact of restraining and driving forces, either anecdotally or by scoring the impact of each force numerically. This will help you identify which forces you should seek to empower or neutralize.

4. Based on the scores, identify which forces the organization can change, influence, or mitigate.

5. Develop a strategy to strengthen driving forces and weaken restraining forces—ideally one that can accomplish both at the same time.

6. Prioritize action steps. Sometimes reducing the restraining forces can be more natural than strengthening the driving forces. Put the most impactful actions at the top of your list.

When a deficit of emotional intelligence appears to be a significant restraining force, you can mitigate this with assessments and training.

Execute Your Transformation Strategy

Each organization's transformation strategy will be different. The strategy will flow from the organization's mission, vision, values, purpose, core competencies, strengths, weaknesses, opportunities, and threats. Leaders will then distill that strategy into tactics and tactics into tasks. This effort involves three complex activities: transitioning tasks, reskilling your workforce, and supporting everyone engaged in the change.

Transition Tasks

The first step in transitioning tasks is to review the tasks included in current job roles and cross-reference these tasks with the capabilities of envisioned and planned automation. This analysis would help determine the shift of workloads from people to machines. Artificial Intelligence (AI) can support this complex process.

Leaders who understand how to allocate tasks to the appropriate resource—an employee, a freelancer, or automation—can develop effective reskilling and recruitment plans. Consider this slogan when you allocate tasks to help you recall your options: build, buy, borrow, or bot.

With so many options for assigning tasks, how can you decide who will do what? Transitioning tasks starts with documenting the required competencies for performing each necessary task, activity, and process and determining whether to assign it to humans or machines. The organization's competency model will help you choose from these four options (Figure 2.3). We will discuss competency models further in Chapter 6.

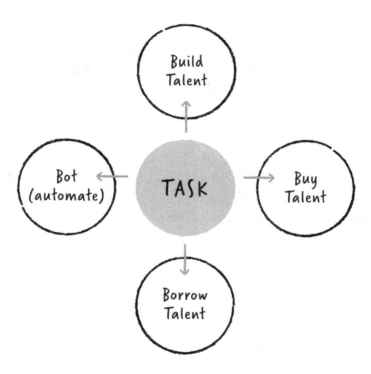

Figure 2.3: Assigning Tasks

Build

Organizations customarily have focused on building their teams by promoting talented employees into new positions; recruiting graduates from schools, colleges, and universities; then using internships, apprenticeships, and onboarding programs to ease newbies into the workplace.

Buy

In addition to building talent from within, organizations have drawn skilled talent from other organizations or worked with outsourcers and recruiters to secure top talent, sometimes luring them with signing bonuses.

Borrow

These days, talent-matching platforms such as Fiverr, Freelancer, and Upwork make it is easy to supplement in-house skills by "borrowing" talent for a few hours or days or on a project-by-project basis. This approach is ideal for short-term assignments such as data entry, building websites, designing graphics, and creating presentations.

Bot

A bot (the term is derived from "robot") is a software application that performs simple and repetitive tasks. The bot acts as a personal assistant. With the advent of AI, bots can model human behaviors to provide useful, meaningful experiences for customers. For example, bots now handle some traditional contact-center tasks: phone calls, email, website chats, text messages, and the like. Yes, bots are artificial, but they can be greatly beneficial.

In Chapter 1, we introduced Robotic Process Automation (RPA), which enables sophisticated forms of bots that automate business processes. RPA systems can "learn" human behavior patterns and replicate them through the use of AI. As an example, employees using RPA to manage a sales and marketing process can rely on AI to detect an exception that requires human intervention. When someone resolves the issue, AI can note this exception and its solution for future reference, as a human would do. As another example, imagine a robotic exoskeleton attached to a person lifting heavy boxes. The exoskeleton gathers data that eventually will enable a machine to mimic that activity and perform the task without human assistance. If this automated worker runs into problems and needs some human intervention, it will nevertheless keep absorbing information that will continue to help it perform better. The result: a robotic "worker" that can toil for twenty-four hours a day, seven days a week, without stopping for coffee or lunch.

Reskill Your Workforce

As automation increasingly takes over mundane and logical tasks and processes, humans will be freer to perform activities that are less predictable, more creative, and increasingly dependent on interpersonal skills. These workers will need reskilling that combines technical training with learning experiences aimed at building new functional skills as well as social skills and emotional intelligence. Through these experiences, they will develop their ability to solve problems, collaborate effectively within dynamic teams, and use emotional intelligence to respond reasonably to new business practices and technologies.

Identify the New Skills Required

Identifying necessary tasks and deciding who will perform them—current employees, freelancers, or bots—will enable you to determine the skills required. Generally speaking, organizations will see less demand for people to use skills involving manual dexterity, physical endurance, precise movement, information recall, and visual inspection. Demand will rise for the ten essential skills we mentioned in Chapter 1: complex problem-solving; critical thinking; creativity; people management; coordinating with others; social, conversational, and emotional intelligence; decision-making; service orientation; negotiation; and cognitive flexibility. Employers also will seek active learners and those who demonstrate originality, initiative, clear communication, social influence, and leadership. Talent for design, development, and systems analysis will be highly desirable.

Training everyone on everything is unlikely to yield the desired outcomes. Here's how to get started on the right track:

- Identify desired outcomes and the tasks required to achieve them.

- Determine the positive and negative forces in play that might support or frustrate the desired outcomes.

- Document the competencies (the behaviors and capabilities) that individuals and teams will need to support the desired outcomes.

- Assess the current competencies available to the individual, team, or organization.

- Perform a gap analysis (Figure 2.4) to pinpoint behaviors and capabilities that require improvement at an organizational, team, and individual level.

- Develop a roadmap to guide the needed talent transformation initiatives.

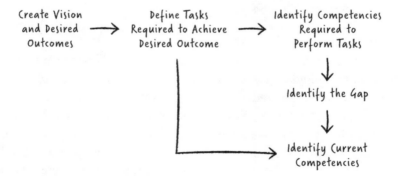

Figure 2.4: Competency Gap Analysis

Assess Current Skills

Assessing skills within the workplace helps identify strengths and weaknesses at an individual, team, or organizational level. Weaknesses might include skills gaps—the differences between people's skills and those required to perform tasks. AI is making it easier to identify these gaps for the short, medium, and long terms and provides useful insights about how to address them.

Assessments are a crucial means of identifying existing skills and helping managers position employees for learning experiences that will enable them to take on roles in the future. Much of this book will explain the role of assessments in talent transformation and offer practical tips for using them effectively.

Provide Learning Opportunities

Once individuals and employers have used assessments to identify skills gaps, they can identify interventions to help employees progress from where they are to where they need to be. Learning opportunities can include in-class or online training, mentoring, apprenticeships, work-study, and other interventions. Systems that use assessment results to provide a "Goldilocks" learning challenge—not too hard or too easy—will accelerate meaningful learning without denting the learner's self-esteem.

Monitor Progress

Regular performance reviews and additional assessments can help individuals and organizations understand the new challenges and new competencies required. Those motivated by this information can engage in new learning opportunities and prepare for roles that meet their career objectives and resonate with their motives, preferences, and values. With new technologies, employees' competencies and preferences can be stored and matched to new opportunities. When it's time to shift jobs, the necessary information will be at hand to identify probable candidates for new roles.

Bring in Freelancers

Organizations are not responsible for developing the skills of gig workers. By identifying skill shortages, talent marketplaces can help freelancers decide which new skills to learn. With the growth of online learning platforms and their cost-effective subscription models, gig workers who respond proactively to skill shortages will be well-positioned to seize opportunities.

Train the Bots

Like other workers, machines and bots need training to do their jobs well. Handing off tasks to technology might require steps as simple as reprogramming. In other cases, people and machines will initially "partner" to perform tasks and manage processes. As they work alongside people, machines will learn from the data these partnerships generate.

Support Everyone Engaged in the Change

Successful talent transformation is not just about meeting future requirements. Understanding the behaviors and capabilities needed during the change process is also critical. The critic, the victim, the disinterested, and the navigator will all need support throughout the transformation. You can use satisfaction surveys, interviews, engagement surveys, and fast and frequent pulse surveys (see Chapter 7) to confirm that initiatives are on course.

Those engaged in change appreciate support that will help them

- understand what management expects of them during the period of change;

- have the information and tools required to support the change;

- have the psychological safety to ensure that challenges are shared and not concealed;

- feel recognized and praised, as reassurance will help speed along the process;

- access caring and supportive structures when they have concerns;

- co-create a future in which learning and development are part of the change process;

- understand the organization's mission, vision, and purpose, even during times of change;

- improve communications and build respect; and

- meet regularly one-on-one with their supervisors and managers to discuss ideas, reflect on progress, and confirm alignment.

Following these simple guidelines will help make the process of change enjoyable, orderly, and refreshing for you and your employees alike.

Takeaways

- Exponential technological progress calls on organizations to embrace the inevitability of change.

- Effective change management requires a vision, objectives, planning, compassion, and effective communication.

- Although some people will cling to the status quo, sensitive handling of emotional responses will engender positive attitudes toward change.

- Once you identify which tasks need doing, you have a choice for allocating them: build, buy, borrow, or bot.

- Workers engaged in change need ongoing support.

3

A HOLISTIC FRAMEWORK
THE TALENT
TRANSFORMATION PYRAMID

WHO HASN'T HEARD a tale of a stellar new hire who outclassed all the other applicants but could not meet the demands of his new job? Or a brilliant developer who fell out with her teammates over a minor disagreement and never reconciled with them? Or that manager who knows the business inside out but is quick to scold colleagues?

In these and countless other cases, you could easily conclude that the person was in some way unfit for their role. You might chalk up shortcomings at work to a lack of skills or an awkward disposition. But that doesn't help you understand what holds people back or help you determine what interventions could help them perform better. You need a more complete view of the person to do that.

That broader perspective helps even before someone starts a new job or gets a promotion. Assessing functional skills in isolation may give you confidence in their ability to perform the tasks listed in their job description. Still, it won't tell you how well they will work with teammates, deal with crises, or adapt to working alongside a robot.

We represent the Talent Transformation Pyramid as a holistic framework for predicting performance, placing people in roles that suit them, and identifying and addressing workplace challenges.

Whether you are trying to solve performance problems, gauge someone's readiness for new responsibilities, or assemble a diverse but compatible team, we believe the Talent Transformation Pyramid will help you evaluate skillsets and mindsets. Then, you can identify specific factors that need your attention and determine what action to take.

How?

- By giving the same weight to emotional intelligence, adaptability, and creative thinking as you do to functional skills and cognitive abilities
- By recognizing that the work situation—encompassing everything from incentives to psychological safety and feelings of inclusion—affects behaviors
- By acknowledging that the work environment—tools, information, job aids, and so forth—can enable or hinder the capabilities of individuals and teams
- By providing a structure for correlating assessment results and potentially determining causation

Most evaluation systems have struggled to integrate the multifaceted elements of performance, but the pyramid brings them together. It enables you to identify the behaviors and capabilities needed for readiness and the learning opportunities that will prepare individuals and teams to achieve results. This approach will become increasingly critical as new jobs and careers emerge along with advanced human-machine interfaces and other technologies.

In this chapter, we introduce the pyramid. First, we identify its components—the twelve factors that most significantly support individual, team, and organizational performance—and we explore their place in the pyramid's hierarchy. We then explain how the factors on lower levels of the pyramid support those that lie above them. We discuss the importance of carefully measuring each factor individually before looking for correlations. Finally, we explain how management dashboards based on the pyramid enable you to evaluate assessment data, analyze metrics, and make sound decisions.

Overview

Graphic models help us understand complex ideas and visualize things we can't see. Think, for example, of Maslow's Hierarchy of Needs or Kirkpatrick's Four Levels of Training Evaluation. Likewise, the Talent Transformation Pyramid helps us think through complex ideas and see the relationships between them. It includes twelve factors that influence organizational performance and aid talent transformation. As you can see in Figure 3.1, the factors appear in triangular building blocks and the horizontal beams that underpin

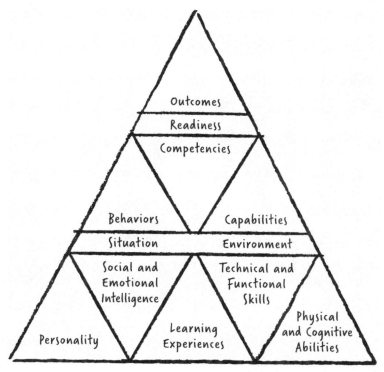

Figure 3.1: The Talent Transformation Pyramid

what lies above them. The pyramid provides the vocabulary and the framework for understanding relationships among these factors.

Notice that the pyramid represents individuals' intrinsic qualities and abilities as well as their emotional intelligence and functional skills. These individual assets underpin the work of teams and, ultimately, of an entire organization. The pyramid

- depicts the factors that support individual, team, and organizational performance and indicates how they relate to each other;

- helps consultants, managers, and other leaders define competencies more strategically;

- helps employers understand the information they need to place employees in the right roles, provide relevant learning experiences for them, and gauge their readiness to perform;

- offers executives, talent managers, consultants, and others a shared vocabulary with which to discuss and agree on the right balance between skills and personal attributes; and

- provides a framework for diagnosing problems and providing interventions, support, and training that will improve performance.

The pyramid is a multidimensional model that you can consider from multiple points of view. You can use it to help organizations, teams, or individuals think through and improve various aspects of readiness and performance.

Finding the right balance between a person's work-related skills and behavioral characteristics will become increasingly critical with the advent of change underpinned by massive automation.

In our quest to upskill and reskill the workforce, we'll need to define both the capabilities and the behaviors required for the new jobs that will emerge. We can then work effectively to identify the individuals best suited for those jobs. In the past, for example, it might have been desirable for individuals in highly technical roles to be able to work independently—even in isolation. However, with increasing automation and specialization, individuals will need to partner with others to make progress. New jobs and careers will demand collaborative approaches to problem-solving, which will require candor, respect, empathy, and understanding as well as curiosity and creativity.

Traditional talent management systems, which fail to integrate the assessment of individuals' human and technical sides, cannot meet these needs. In contrast, the pyramid considers behaviors and capabilities together—along with their supporting factors—to help leaders, managers, and individuals manage the transitions that are coming with increased automation.

The Twelve Factors That Support Performance

Like a physical pyramid, the Talent Transformation Pyramid incorporates individual elements. Each block and beam is essential, but the connections within the complete structure provide reinforcement, stability, and strength. As you work with the pyramid, you can focus on one factor or consider several that might interact within your organization.

Ahead are basic definitions of the factors that support performance, along with a brief explanation of how the factors influence each other. We'll work through the left side of the pyramid, which represents mindset, before looking at technical and functional skills. But first, let's explore the center of the pyramid's foundation to consider learning experiences, which impact both mindset and skillset.

Learning experiences (Figure 3.2) are exposures to, participation in, or observations of events, actions, and personal interactions that promote learning. They can be formal or informal. These learning experiences inform and generally improve our emotional intelligence and functional skills.

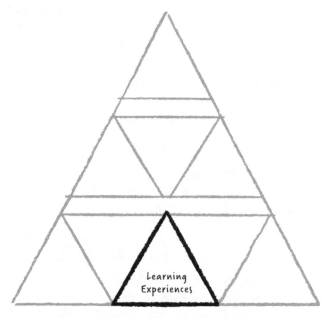

Figure 3.2: Learning Experiences

Factors Contributing to Mindset

Mindset (Figure 3.3) affects our creativity, adaptability, social awareness, emotional intelligence, and interactions with others. Our personality, values, preferences, motivations, and life experiences underpin our emotional and social intelligence. Formal and informal learning teach us social and emotional intelligence, which develop mindset. Our behaviors depend not only on our skills but also on the situation in which we find ourselves. Examples of

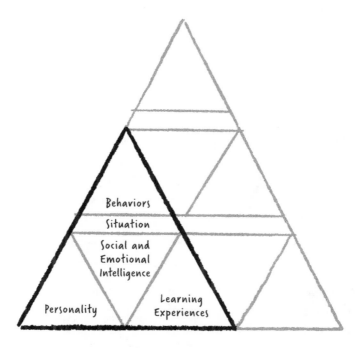

Figure 3.3: Mindset

behaviors we might exhibit include flexibility, diligence, responsiveness, engagement, dependability, candor, empathy, and respect.
With organizations relying increasingly on teams to solve problems
and execute strategy, we need to pay more attention to mindset than
ever before.

Personality (Figure 3.4) includes an individual's traits, values,
motives, and preferences. It incorporates characteristic patterns of
thinking, feeling, and behaving. Experts say our personalities form
by the age of eight and rarely change unless we experience a life
crisis such as a near-death experience or the loss of a loved one. To
a certain extent, our personality sets the baseline for our level of
emotional intelligence.

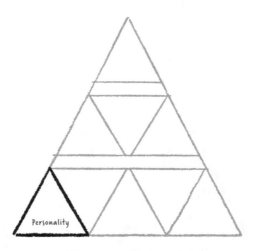

Figure 3.4: Personality

Social and emotional intelligence (Figure 3.5) is the capacity to be aware of, control, and express emotions and to handle relationships effectively. Social and emotional intelligence helps us understand others' feelings, motives, and behaviors, as well as our own. If someone is bullying teammates, an emotionally intelligent person would

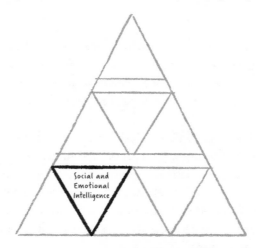

Figure 3.5: Social and Emotional Intelligence

respond maturely to the intimidating behavior. While our personality might give us some built-in emotional intelligence, we can also develop it through informal learning experiences. For instance, a teenager might figure out the value of keeping one's cool after getting into a needless shouting match. We can also learn emotional intelligence through formal educational courses. Regardless of how we learn it, emotional intelligence enables us to behave effectively in the workplace, even if our underlying personality might make us inclined to act differently.

Situation (Figure 3.6) can be considered a set of circumstances that support or undermine behaviors. In the workplace, the situation includes everything from workplace culture and behavioral norms to pay, incentives, and benefits such as health insurance and paid vacations. It also takes account of inclusion and psychological safety—the extent to which we feel we can voice our concerns, ask questions, admit mistakes, and ask for help. Just as with physical

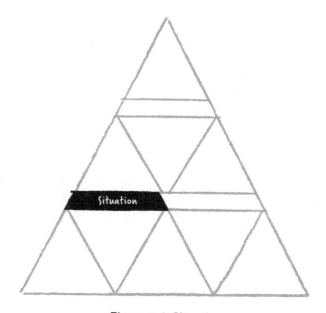

Figure 3.6: Situation

safety, psychological safety helps workers perform their jobs well and bolster each other's readiness to perform. Positive elements in our situation—say a genuinely caring boss who is always open to feedback—help us behave as expected and perform well. A negative workplace undermines our behavior. Financial incentives such as bonuses, commissions, or other perks can have a positive impact on performance, but only if they encourage honest work. Financial scandals often start with ill-conceived incentives.

Questions to Help You Discover the Root Cause of Workplace Stress

- Do an individual's personality traits, values, motives, and preferences support the behaviors expected on the job?

- Does someone have to draw so much upon social and emotional intelligence that it increases their job-related stress?

- Are there people whose personalities resonate with their jobs, but who nevertheless land in situations where they struggle to behave appropriately?

- Do the incentives we have in place encourage behaviors that resonate with the organization's values?

- Are we providing the right level of psychological safety for team members?

Behaviors (Figure 3.7) are the ways people act in various circumstances. In other words, they are situation dependent. For example, we are likely to be rambunctious at a football game but sit silently at the symphony. At work, we behave in a systematic way that fits in with our company's culture. We might be punctual, for example, or focus closely on results, or work well within a team. Work situations and surroundings can influence behaviors, both positively and negatively.

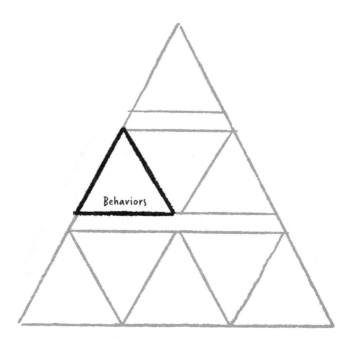

Figure 3.7: Behaviors

Factors Contributing to Skillset

Skillset (Figure 3.8) represents the specific cognitive and physical skills we need to perform a particular task or job successfully. We acquire skills through formal and informal learning experiences. These experiences could include school, college, apprenticeships, training programs, coaching, online courses, and on-the-job training.

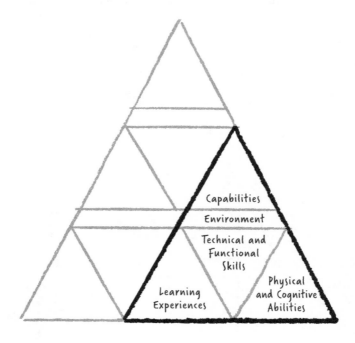

Figure 3.8: Skillset

Some consultants use the term "half-life of skills" to represent how the value of a skill declines over time. The half-lives of skills will shorten as the workplace adopts new technologies more rapidly, causing workers to update their skillsets continuously.

Skillsets include activities such as using, designing, building, repairing, editing, calculating, measuring, analyzing, investigating, and testing.

Physical and cognitive abilities (Figure 3.9) involve the body and mind. Physical abilities include movement, balance, and coordination, whereas cognitive abilities include learning, memorizing, reasoning, and problem-solving. The functional skills we learn through formal and informal experiences build on our physical and cognitive abilities.

For many job roles, physical abilities rarely prevent an individual from performing well. However, some professions, such as firefighting, require specific physical abilities.

Cognitive abilities, also known as general mental capabilities, include comprehending complex ideas, learning from experience, planning, reasoning, problem-solving, and abstract thinking.

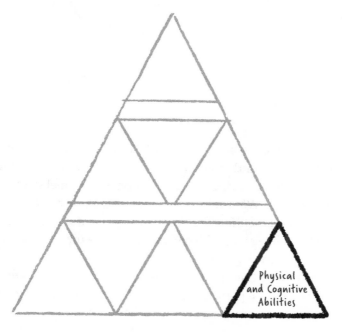

Figure 3.9: Physical and Cognitive Abilities

Technical and functional skills (Figure 3.10) are the motor-mechanical and cognitive skills that we have learned and possess to

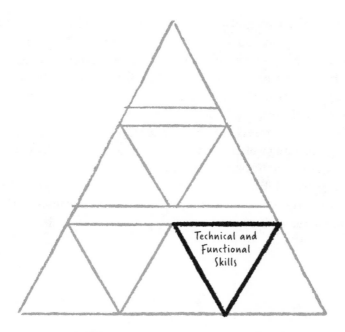

Figure 3.10: Technical and Functional Skills

perform specific tasks. We use our physical and cognitive abilities—aided by formal and informal learning experiences—to develop these skills. In early childhood, functional skills include learning to walk and talk. Work-related skills might include driving a tractor or writing a marketing plan. Whatever their nature, technical and functional skills—along with our environment—dictate how capable we are of performing tasks.

Environment (Figure 3.11) is the physical setting in which an individual or team performs a task, whether it is replacing an electric motor or detecting a fraudulent banknote. The environment includes elements such as information, job aids, tools, workspace, air quality, noise level, and lighting. Comfortable, well-equipped environments enhance people's capabilities and encourage higher levels of performance. If we were assembling a bookshelf at night

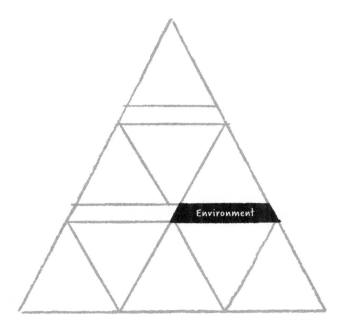

Figure 3.11: Environment

and the lights went out, we'd have a hard time getting this task done even if we were old hands at building furniture. Likewise, a top-notch business analyst would lose ground if they had to use an outdated computer.

Capabilities (Figure 3.12) are the tasks that an individual or team is capable of doing, given the functional skills, tools, information, and job aids available to them while performing the task. Your in-house statistics whiz will perform far better using the latest software than they will on the 2003 version. Conversely, someone with no database training or experience will get little done even with the newest system. In either case, each worker will underperform. Capabilities deploy both functional skills and physical and cognitive abilities. The work environment, as well as someone's ability level, will influence their success or failure.

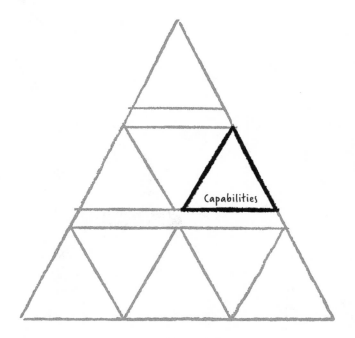

Figure 3.12: Capabilities

Questions for Discovering the Root Cause of Inadequate Performance

- Are we providing sufficient and appropriate learning experiences to transfer skills to the individual?

- Do individuals have the right functional skills to perform their assigned tasks safely and appropriately?

- Are we giving individuals access to the right tools, information, job aids, and physical environment for performing the tasks required?

Environments matter.

Competencies (Figure 3.13) document the behaviors and capabilities required to complete a task. The term can also refer to a record or assertion of an individual's or team's capabilities. There are behavior-related competencies (teamwork and confidentiality, for example) and capability-related competencies (such as truck driving or JavaScript programming). Competencies bring together everything we see beneath them in the pyramid. Taking account of everything from physical and cognitive abilities and personality to behaviors and capabilities helps organizations identify competencies that will meet their changing needs. And once they define a competency, leaders can look down through the pyramid to determine why an individual or team may have failed to achieve it. Competency models document and group competencies together to describe required behaviors and capabilities in addition to the necessary performance environment and the levels of potential performance. We'll discuss competency models in Chapter 6.

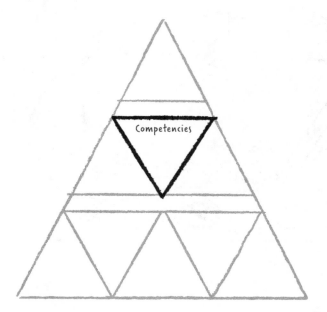

Figure 3.13: Competencies

Questions to Ask about Competencies

- How should we document the capabilities required to perform the essential tasks of the job?

- In documenting the required behaviors and capabilities, have we set expectations at the right level (e.g., not too detailed but not too superficial)?

- Do our competency definitions help individuals determine how to improve their behaviors and capabilities?

- How will we accumulate evidence to help us determine behaviors and capabilities?

- Have we appropriately documented evidence or assertions of an individual's actual behaviors and capabilities?

A Behavioral Competency

Competency Name: Teamwork

Competency Definition: To be able to complete tasks while coordinating and collaborating with others

Desired Behaviors:

- Stay committed to the team's objectives.

- Facilitate team interaction.

- Delegate necessary tasks.

- Collaborate—utilizing each other's strengths and mitigating each other's weaknesses to complete tasks.

Continued...

- Handle conflicts effectively.

- Stay open to group opinions and suggestions.

- Motivate group members to submit ideas.

- Support and follow group decisions.

- Effectively handle work-style differences.

A Capability Competency

Competency Name: Install and Configure a Model XL Router

Competency Definition: To be able to install a Model XL Router within a 19-inch rack and securely configure it for route IP traffic on an internal network.

Required Skills:
- Determine that the work area is safe.

- Determine whether to install the new router in a "hot" or "cold" rack.

- Take the necessary precautions if installing the router in a hot rack.

- Install the router into the rack safely and securely.

- Apply power to the rack and ensure that it powers up correctly.

- Use configuration software to ensure that the router passes all internal diagnostic tests.

- Use configuration software to configure and route IP traffic securely on an internal network.

- Insert network cables and run security tests to ensure the router is performing correctly.

Readiness (Figure 3.14) is the degree to which an individual, team, or organization is prepared to perform effectively. At the organizational and team levels, readiness has to do with strategy, mission, goals, customer needs, competitive landscape, resources, leadership, budgets, support functions, and more. At an individual level, readiness applies to the behaviors and capabilities required to achieve the person's specific objectives. An individual can use the model to determine which behaviors and capabilities they should be developing to be ready for their next promotion. Being able to predict performance is crucial for allocating resources, developing behaviors and capabilities, and achieving favorable performance outcomes. The question is, "Are we ready to perform?" And if not, "What do we need to make ourselves ready?"

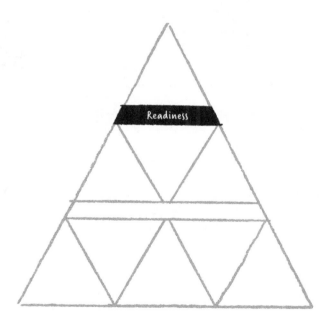

Figure 3.14: Readiness

Outcomes (Figure 3.15) are the result of executing one or more tasks; the degree to which an individual, team, or organization succeeds at a given task or role. We measure performance outcomes with a variety of metrics. At an organizational level, we might use Key Performance Indicators (KPIs), Objectives and Key Results (OKRs), balanced scorecards, satisfaction ratings, or financial metrics such as revenue, profit/loss, and return on investment. For individuals, we might consider revenue generated, customer satisfaction, customers served, training delivered, and other metrics that the person affected. These historical metrics reflect what has already happened, but they also provide valuable data that can inform decision-making that promotes future readiness.

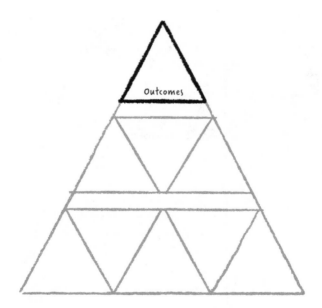

Figure 3.15: Outcomes

Arranging the Factors to Reveal Connections

The twelve factors in the Talent Transformation Pyramid appear hierarchically and from side to side to show how they relate to each other. Once we understand these relationships, we can more effectively develop interventions that enable readiness and performance. This understanding will be increasingly crucial as tasks become more complex and teamwork more central to organizations' performance.

Building Success from the Ground Up

The factors in the bottom layer of the pyramid, as shown in Figure 3.16, relate to individuals. In the middle layer, individuals become teams. The top layer brings individuals and teams into the organizational view for a look at readiness and actual performance.

Assessments play a crucial role in measuring the factors at all levels of the pyramid. The following chapters provide details on how to assess the various factors for individuals, teams, and organizations.

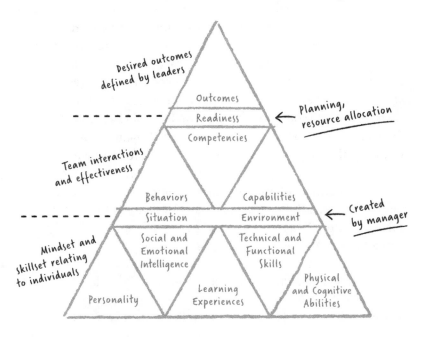

Figure 3.16: Layers of the Pyramid

Individual Knowledge, Skills, and Abilities

The left side of the pyramid's foundation focuses on individuals' personal characteristics related to interpersonal skills. There, we assess personality (traits, values, motives, and preferences) and social and emotional intelligence. We also evaluate the impact of an individual's work situation on their behaviors. On the right side, we concentrate on cognitive and physical abilities as well as technical and functional skills. It's essential to bear in mind that someone's capabilities depend not only on their technical and functional skills but also on the environment in which they perform their tasks. At the center of it all, formal and informal learning experiences help people build both their mindset and skillset.

Team Interactions and Effectiveness

The middle layer of the pyramid applies to individuals and their work within teams. That is, individuals' behaviors and capabilities contribute to the behaviors and capabilities of their teams. These behaviors and capabilities can be documented and asserted at an individual or team level using a competency management system.

Individuals within a team need to trust one another to be successful. As Patrick Lencioni describes in his book *The Five Dysfunctions of a Team*, trust among team members enables authentic conversations that lead to commitment, accountability, and a focus on results. Trust greatly enhances team behaviors, which include how members work together to get things done, use their resources, and achieve results. These factors, in turn, support the team's effectiveness.

In the context of massive automation, it will be crucial to understand an individual's and a team's openness to the demands for reskilling. Gauging attitudes toward change will help guide employee engagement and training programs.

Organizational Readiness and Performance

At the top of the pyramid, we're looking at an entire organization as well as individuals and teams. Individuals, teams, and organizations that are well prepared and understand expectations and requirements will be ready to perform and will achieve positive performance outcomes. Measuring these outcomes provides retrospective data we can use as we aim for improvement. This data will also inform future upskilling and reskilling initiatives.

Questions to Ask while Appraising Readiness

- Have we established and communicated our strategies and goals effectively?

- Are we planning for success with the right levels of resource allocation?

- Have we developed contingency plans to take account of the potential variants of the circumstances we might encounter?

- Do we understand the issues that we will need to address, such as competitors, as we progress?

Looking at Both Sides

A central premise of the pyramid is the importance of giving as much attention to mindset as to skillset. The left and right sides of the pyramid present the factors related to these two aspects of every person—facets that are brought together within competencies.

Left-hand Side—Behavioral Supports

The left-hand side of the pyramid is about behaviors. Behaviors are rooted in personality, an individual's current situation, and the social and emotional intelligence they have developed. However, learning and life experience influence behaviors too (Figure 3.17). A discordant team engenders stress, requiring members to rely on their social and emotional intelligence to behave as their job requires. Conversely, a strong but sympathetic boss and cooperative employees will work together effectively.

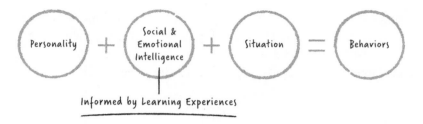

Figure 3.17: Factors That Support Behaviors

Right-hand Side—Support for Capabilities

The right side of the pyramid is about capabilities, which are rooted in technical and functional skills (Figure 3.18). An individual's skill-set also relies on physical and cognitive abilities, along with formal and informal learning. A person's working environment strongly influences their capabilities.

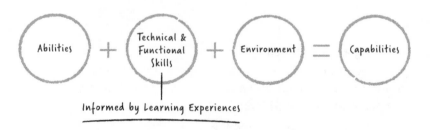

Figure 3.18: Factors That Support Capabilities

Deborah has had challenging bosses before, but these days she's under tremendous stress. Her boss, Natalie, micromanages every project, despite Deborah's success as a systems developer. Natalie roams the floor and peers over Deborah's shoulder, critiquing her work at every step. Deborah is fighting the instinct to tell Natalie to get lost! Although she has learned from years of working under pressure that losing her temper would be counterproductive, she also recognizes that spending so much energy to maintain her composure could reduce her job performance.

Micromanaging creates stress.

Bringing It All Together

The twelve factors are crucial to performance, even when considered individually. However, just as weaving lengths of delicate fiber produces sturdy cloth, the factors gain power and strength from each other.

How Factors Support Each Other

At each level of the pyramid, the triangular blocks and horizontal beams support those above them.

Readiness Supports Outcomes

Again, readiness is the degree to which an organization is fully prepared for something. Whereas outcomes look back at what has already happened, readiness predicts future performance.

Readiness (Figure 3.19) reflects how well stakeholders are aligned to achieve an organization's mission, vision, and purpose. This factor requires effective planning, resource allocation, and operational tactics based on an understanding of an organization's strengths, weaknesses, opportunities, and threats.

If we don't know that an individual, team, or organization is ready, we can't predict performance outcomes.

Figure 3.19: Readiness Supporting Outcomes

Behaviors and Capabilities Support Readiness

The behaviors and capabilities needed to perform a task (Figure 3.20) support a person's readiness to do it well. Well-written competencies define the behaviors and capabilities required for success. Competency definitions can provide a benchmark for evaluating the degree to which an individual, team, or organization is ready to perform the tasks required. Without high marks for behaviors, capabilities, and thoughtful planning, readiness is hard to come by.

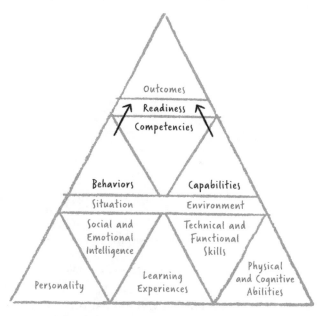

Figure 3.20: Behaviors and Capabilities
Supporting Readiness and Outcomes

Situation Should Support Desirable Behaviors

The workplace culture, norms, incentives, and other aspects of the situation (Figure 3.21) can affect how individuals and teams behave. A positive, respectful workplace in which employees feel safe and cared for begets desirable behaviors. Everything should work smoothly if the work situation is engineered to support the behaviors a job requires. These include not only the task-related behaviors, but also the creativity, resilience, communication, and discipline involved.

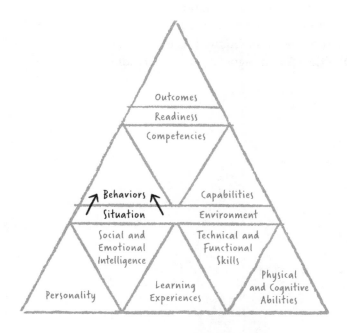

Figure 3.21: Situation Supports Behaviors

Unfortunately, aspects of the work situation can often undermine the expected behaviors instead of supporting them. In such cases, social and emotional intelligence comes into play. For example, suppose Marco's job in customer support requires him to keep his cool, but his supervisor's aggressive manner makes him feel nervous and uneasy. Marco will need to use his emotional intelligence to restrain his desire to respond with defensiveness or anger to his boss, a coworker, or a customer. That internal effort to keep calm will sap Marco's energy. He'll behave as he should, but at a cost.

Environment Should Support Capabilities

The tools in use, information available, job aids, and the physical environment (air quality, noise, light, and workspace configuration; Figure 3.22) affect how individuals and teams perform tasks. Workers required to complete jobs in adverse environments need specialized training to enable them to cope with these conditions. In addition to the physical environment, the information, tools, and job aids that workers have access to—as well as their proficiency in using them—will affect their capabilities.

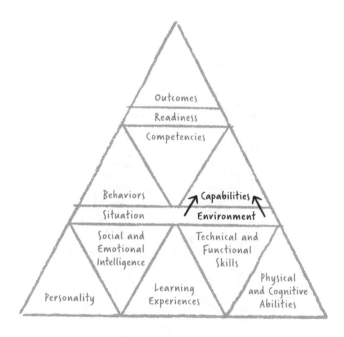

Figure 3.22: Environment Supports Capabilities

Jean, a nurse, was taking nasal swabs for COVID-19 testing in a drive-through clinic. Personal Protective Equipment (PPE) enabled her to work safely. She used a tablet to enter patient details and access information to share with her patients. It was cold that day, so she wore warm clothing to stay comfortable and avoid shivering. Taking swabs needed a steady hand. Jean had a reputation for efficiency and cheerfulness, but she was short-tempered that day. Her shift was supposed to end an hour ago, and the clinic hadn't told her who would take over. She longed to go inside to escape the cold, but she cared about the people waiting in line. She'd stay on the job until it was time to leave, but she was not doing her best work. Jean couldn't help thinking that if she had to endure many more days like this, she might have to start looking for a new job.

The environment can impact capabilities.

For Easier Measurement, Isolate Each Factor

As we have said, the pyramid's first layer of factors includes the basic building blocks for individual competence. We need to assess how valid and reliable the data is from each of these factors individually, learning as much as we can about each before exploring how it correlates to other factors. When we can trust that the data from each factor is valid and reliable, we can start to investigate correlation using data harvested from other factors. Once we've observed a correlation between factors, we can investigate further to identify the root cause.

Imagine we have three sales teams in different cities—Chicago, Miami, and Los Angeles—selling a new virtual conferencing platform. Chicago's numbers are through the roof, but the other two teams are in the doldrums. Before we leap to the potentially invalid conclusion that talent is the issue here, we should look at how various external factors match up. External factors could be competition, marketing, product suitability, and the like. The more data we can reference, the more insightful our conclusions will be.

In tandem with looking at external factors, we can look at talent-related factors. All three teams have been through similar recruitment processes and training courses. None of them have been through training on social and emotional intelligence, but assessments conducted during recruitment indicated that all three teams possess similar personality and emotional quotients (EQ).

Is the challenge related to the teams' behaviors or their capabilities? When we examine pulse survey data to determine levels of employee satisfaction, incentives, benefits, and tools, a couple of orange flags show up. Salespeople are less satisfied in Miami than in Chicago, and the Miamians have criticized the product. After digging further into the survey data, we discover that the Los Angeles team is also disgruntled, but we don't know why. What's the source of their dissatisfaction?

We can see a correlation here, but is it the product itself that is causing unhappiness and poor performance in both Miami and Los Angeles? We'd better do some interviews!

Data can shine some light into the darkness, but a series of interviews can quickly distinguish between valid and invalid hypotheses. Conversations reveal that in Miami, the conferencing platform is not available in Spanish. That's not an issue for the Los Angeles team, but here's what's been bugging them: Their tyrannical boss is setting the sales staff on edge. The staff in Los Angeles fear potential consequences from complaining about their boss. No wonder it was hard to detect the source of their angst within the survey data.

This journey started by looking at performance outcomes data: Two groups were down, and one was flying high. We had to determine which data, from which factors, correlated with these differences in performance. With correlations established, it was possible to drill down further into the real cause of the problem. In our example, two different factors affected performance. One case revolved around product shortcomings, whereas the other had to do with strained relationships.

Gather Data about Each Factor into Dashboards

While it's crucial to isolate each factor to measure it effectively, it's also essential to bring together all the information you've collected.

Gathering data about all the factors for dashboards enables you to evaluate assessment data, analyze metrics, and make sound decisions.

A car's dashboard provides useful indicators about speed, fuel, engine performance, and tire pressures. Likewise, an organization's information dashboard tracks KPIs that can provide insights into a broad array of performance outcomes, systems, and processes. Dashboards, and their data visualizations, can simplify voluminous data to draw attention to specific issues that might need attention.

Talent dashboards generally display vital information related to recruitment, performance, succession, learning, certifications, and compensation. Talent Transformation dashboards can also provide a holistic view for organizations going through digital transformations.

Competition and financial pressure will drive organizations to automate their business using Artificial Intelligence (AI), Machine

Learning (ML), Robotic Process Automation (RPA), the Internet of Things (IoT), and new devices. As organizations scale up their automation, a unique style of talent dashboard will become essential to promote understanding and manage talent transformation. There are two manifestations of these transitions:

1. Organizations will need to involve employees in "training" the robot that will take on some of their tasks.

2. As automation starts to take on employees' tasks, responsible organizations will track how they can reskill and upskill employees to perform new tasks.

Robots can learn from humans.

Dashboards underpinned by advanced analytics will help us manage these two issues, thereby improving recruiting, onboarding, training, development, and talent transitions. Using automation at scale, we will be able to analyze data and detect correlations. From there, we can seek to determine causation and then consider appropriate interventions. With trustable data, analytics, and dashboards, leaders and managers will be able to make effective decisions and work through transitions and transformations successfully. Using technology to help identify required interventions will lead to improved readiness and performance and thus build a more robust organization.

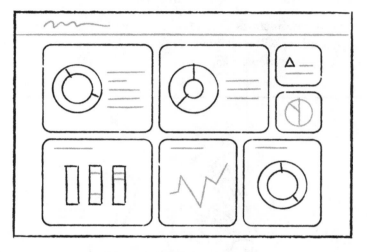

Dashboards bring factors together.

Takeaways

- The Talent Transformation Pyramid focuses on the factors that support performance.

- Although behaviors and capabilities support readiness and performance, non-talent-related issues also have an impact.

- Measuring the factors individually and then correlating the results can help you determine where interventions would be valuable.

ASSESSMENTS—PAST, PRESENT, AND FUTURE

SSESSMENTS ARE POTENT predictors of readiness and performance. They help us gauge the likelihood of a successful
outcome. We can assume that someone who has passed a
driving test is more likely to follow the rules of the road and
drive more safely than someone who hasn't. A customer satisfaction survey gives us a good sense of how likely customers will be to
return and buy more.

Assessments help individuals, teams, and organizations predict behaviors and performance and promote learning and change.
Assessments also can help individuals formulate a plan to develop
their skills by revealing their personality traits, strengths, leadership
style, social personas, emotional intelligence, and functional skills.
Using the right assessment instruments, tools, and services at the
right time and in the proper context provides information leaders
can use to promote harmony and performance in the workplace.

This chapter recalls the history of assessments, explains their
value to society, discusses their current uses, notes some best practices for ensuring that assessments measure the right things, and
peeks at changes to come.

The Evolution of Assessments

Assessments have a long history as tools for promoting learning, training, and personnel management. We believe assessments will become even more significant, with surveys, quizzes, tests, and exams playing a crucial role in helping individuals, teams, and organizations keep abreast of exponential change. Just as new technologies have already driven progress in assessment, they will continue to do so during this new age of massive-scale automation and digital transformation.

Ancient Assessments

The history of assessments confirms the adage that there's nothing new under the sun.

As far back as the Han dynasty in China (206 BC–AD 220), candidates for the civil service took exams to prove their knowledge and demonstrate their potential. If your local prefect recommended you for a clerical job, you had to show that you could memorize thousands of Chinese characters. If you were in line for a higher position, the emperor himself might conduct an oral test to measure your knowledge of policy issues. Although an aristocrat or local official would have nominated you for a post, ostensibly because you were smart and had a good reputation, testing would confirm your suitability for the job.

These ancient Chinese imperial examinations grew into a multitiered system that lasted until 1905. Influenced by the Chinese approach, other Asian nations gradually set up testing systems too. The Western world took note. The British East India Company, founded in 1600, administered tests to select employees, and the British government started screening tests for prospective civil servants in 1855. The United States set up testing for specific government jobs in 1883.

Increased Demand for Tests of Knowledge and Skills

Plato promoted education as a means of achieving justice around 375 BC in his dialogue "The Republic," and the Aztecs of Mexico introduced a system of compulsory education of all children in the fifteenth century. Educational testing, as we know it today, took hold in the nineteenth century during the Second Industrial Revolution, when young people were leaving farms and taking up industrial jobs.

Although some countries enacted compulsory education laws in the nineteenth century, the United States did not make public education mandatory until the early 1920s. More schools meant more testing, but grading papers by hand was time-consuming and tedious. By the mid-twentieth century, machine-readable bubble sheets and optical scanners eased the grind of grading tests—which meant that teachers could give more tests!

In the 1990s, software for creating and administering tests and other assessments swiftly made the use of online surveys, quizzes, tests, and exams a kingpin of many education and training programs. By then, employers had responded to sophisticated processes and complex technologies by documenting competency models to ensure that workers adjusted to these changes. Tests and exams would confirm, as they do today, employees' knowledge and abilities, especially in areas related to health, safety, and compliance. And today, assessments play a crucial role in recruiting, onboarding, professional development, certification, and coaching.

See Chapter 6 for a discussion of competency models.

Assessing Personalities

Although personality testing emerged at the turn of the twentieth century, it came to the fore in the 1990s. The ability of personality testing to tease out underlying traits made it a popular tool for recruiting and selecting job candidates. Organizations training their employees to work effectively in teams began using assessment instruments and learning resources designed specifically to help people develop emotional intelligence, understanding, and respect.

Our interest in psychology has a long history that dates back to the ancient Greeks. However, psychology did not emerge as a separate discipline until the late 1800s, notably when William James described in *The Principles of Psychology* a link between our internal psychological state and our behaviors and environment.

The understanding of psychology and personality soared during the twentieth century. Behaviorists—including B.F. Skinner and John Watson—examined how experiences, rewards, and punishments affected behaviors. Supported by statistics and the use of control groups, the science of assessing personalities advanced in the 1930s. The academic journal *Character and Personality* attracted contributions from Alfred Adler and Carl Jung. Other significant contributors to an understanding of personality were American psychologists Gordon Allport and Henry Murray and English-born Raymond Cattell.

In the fifties and sixties, senior-level managers and executives often underwent projective measures such as the Rorschach Test and the Thematic Apperception Test (TAT). These measures were rarely used for other prospective employees because they were labor-intensive and required a trained psychologist to interpret the test taker's responses. These tests helped psychologists evaluate creativity, problem-solving strategies, interpersonal relationships, and ability to manage ambiguity. Many more people take equivalent tests today since sophisticated software can now interpret the results—a big plus when jobs increasingly require intellectual rather than physical work.

Today we understand personality as an individual's patterns of thought, feeling, and behavior. When we discuss personality in this book, we mean personality traits, preferences, values, and motives.

The post–World War II era brought theories of personality traits and the relationship between specific traits and sub-traits. Under the widely accepted Big Five personality trait theory—which was recently expanded to the Big Six, as discussed further in Chapter 6—

psychologists have identified the traits that most significantly impact our behaviors:

- Honesty-humility
- Emotionality
- Extraversion
- Agreeableness
- Conscientiousness
- Openness to experience

Psychologists also came to recognize that adults' personality traits tend to stay constant over time. Thus, it would be possible to develop personality tests that could predict the probability of employees behaving in particular ways given specific situations. Although some types of personality tests have been in use since the turn of the twentieth century, many organizations embraced them in the 1990s as a means of screening and selecting job candidates. Today, assessing traits, values, preferences, and motivations helps many organizations predict job-fit and team-fit and guides management and executive coaching.

Deploying Assessments at Scale

Thanks to technology, some organizations have accumulated massive datasets and can calculate norms regarding the personality traits, values, motives, and preferences best suited to a role. With the increased use of technology to determine an assessment's validity and reliability, organizations can confidently deploy personality tests and other behavioral-style assessments at scale.

The assessment of technical and functional skills, as well as physical and cognitive abilities, has also grown dramatically. In the 1990s, the increasing complexity of workplace tasks and the need to demonstrate compliance made it necessary to deploy more assessments at scale. And the technology was available to do this: The ubiquity of desktop and laptop computers, combined with the growth of the Internet, made it possible to test more and more people. Since then, technological progress has streamlined delivery of tests and exams for recruiting and onboarding, and for conducting internal and external certifications.

How Are Assessments Used Today?

As we have seen, the science of measuring personalities as well as functional skills has matured so much that it can now help organizations provide more trustworthy assessment results. Within organizations, executives, managers, and other leaders now use assessments at every stage of work, from recruitment through executive development. Some assessments are formative, reinforcing learning in real time. Others are diagnostic, identifying knowledge and skills gaps that appropriate interventions can remedy. Summative assessments measure knowledge at the end of a course or as part of a certification process. Personality and behavioral tests come in various shapes and sizes to determine job-fit or team-fit, or to provide feedback for personal development.

While no single assessment can accurately describe a person's fitness for a job, several assessments together can create a pretty clear picture. The results of surveys, quizzes, and tests can provide valuable evidence of a candidate's capabilities and suitability for a role. Assessment results can drive not only the selection of job candidates but also many other organizational actions and interventions. If assessments suggest that employee morale is low, for example, the executive team could circulate messages to promote understanding and boost people's energy. If there is conflict among colleagues, you might provide opportunities to learn about social and emotional intelligence. Faced with poor performance, you could offer more job aids, information, or better tools. If profitability is lagging, you should look at pricing, review your customer satisfaction ratings, and keep investigating until you discover what is going on. Once you have intervened, you can see whether things have changed for the better.

In this section, we'll provide examples of myriad ways to use assessments.

Recruitment, Selection, and Promotion

Using a variety of assessments can help you determine how closely a candidate's competencies, behaviors, and capabilities match the job's requirements. You can use assessments in conjunction with interviews to reduce the impact of bias and help everyone focus on required behaviors and skills.

Assessments that help determine selection, job placement, and promotion must relate to the competencies, behaviors, and capabilities required for each role. Here are some examples:

- **Abstract Reasoning:** measures problem-solving skills and the ability to recognize patterns and visual cognition. Participants must answer a series of multiple-choice questions in a limited time.

- **Accuracy:** evaluates the ability to provide deliverables accurately and on time. The assessment might present a challenge to perform several tasks within a set timeframe and with a certain level of accuracy. This test might also determine how well a person can multitask under pressure.

- **Attention to Detail:** measures how well a candidate will be aware of, and understands, details.

- **Cognitive Ability:** measures a candidate's ability to think; typically assesses logical, verbal, and numerical reasoning.

- **Computer Literacy:** measures a candidate's computer skills and comfort level using a computer; tests their knowledge of web browsers, software suites, and more.

- **Emotional Intelligence:** measures how well someone understands themselves and others and how likely they are to build relationships with others.

- **Functional Skills:** measures the level of competency for specific industry skills.

- **Integrity:** assesses personality traits associated with integrity, such as conscientiousness, thereby helping organizations hire honest, reliable, and disciplined individuals.

- **Job Knowledge:** measures a candidate's knowledge of and ability to perform the tasks required of a specific role.

- **Keyboard Skills:** combines with computer literacy tests to measure typing speed, precision, and accuracy. Keyboard tests are particularly relevant for jobs that require crunching high volumes of data.

- **Language—Listening Comprehension:** tests a candidate's ability to hear, understand information, and detect a speaker's verbal cues.

- **Language—Reading Comprehension:** tests a candidate's ability to deduce information from a written document. The individual's answers to questions about each passage reveal their understanding of it. The selection often does not suggest answers directly, requiring the candidate to demonstrate reasoning skills.

- **Language—Verbal:** checks a person's comfort level in speaking, their ability to communicate clearly, and their choice of phrases and words.

- **Language—Written:** tests punctuation usage, application of correct grammar, word usage, the ability to differentiate between homonyms, grasp of basic salutations, and so on.

- **Learning Ability:** measures the candidate's ability to learn the knowledge and cognitive skills required to perform the tasks of a role.

- **Numeracy Skills (Basic):** presents puzzles, questions, and patterns that call for quick mental arithmetic. Often the questions are timed so that the candidate must solve the puzzles quickly.

- **Numeracy Skills (Advanced):** might require finding a solution from reading tables of data and charts. This advanced assessment usually allows slightly more time per question and the use of calculators.

- **Personality Traits:** evaluates how well someone would fit within an organization or team based on the candidate's core values, motivations, temperament, preferences, and other personality traits.

- **Physical Ability:** evaluates physical abilities required for jobs that require strength, stamina, and agility by having the candidate perform physical tasks such as carrying a weight over a distance.

- **Retention:** determines an individual's ability to retain information, data, and skills. Versions of this test may work as a memory game, presenting several images, layouts, graphics, and information one after the other and then asking questions about them in random order.

- **Situational Judgment Assessment (SJA):** presents work-relevant situations that often involve dilemmas and asks participants to judge possible responses. These assessments are useful in onboarding, training, development, and certification to ascertain whether an employee's sense of judgment will align with best practices and regulations.

Sample Question for Assessing Situational Judgment

You work in a bank, and you know you must have a customer's proper identification before helping them with financial transactions. Although the customer does not have a suitable photo ID, a senior executive insists that you perform the transaction.

What would you do?

A   Concede to the executive's demand, as you don't want to lose your job.

B   Ask the customer to wait and then ask your manager for advice.

C   Ask the customer to return with a photo ID.

D   Ask to use the executive's photo ID for identification purposes.

- **Spatial Awareness:** requires the candidate to visualize 2D and 3D objects in space and identify how an object would look from another perspective. These assessments apply to roles involving managing and maintaining machines, design, engineering, and architectural skills.

- **Speed Assessment:** assesses a person's speed in performing role-related tasks, using hands-on assessments or simulated scenarios.

Onboarding, Training, and Professional Development

Effective onboarding and training have a tremendous impact on workforce productivity and employee retention. Assessments help organizations shape new employees' impressions and establish a clear understanding of expectations. In turn, these assessments help new hires understand their new environment and contribute more quickly than they would otherwise.

Assessments—used in conjunction with conversations and interviews—help deepen understanding between colleagues, supervisors, and managers:

- **Behavioral Style Assessments:** help new employees understand their behavioral style and its implications within the workplace. Two of the most popular assessments in this category are the Myers–Briggs Type Indicator (MBTI) and DISC, which measures Dominance, Influence, Steadiness, and Conscientiousness.

- **Competence Exams:** measures knowledge, skills, and abilities.

- **Course Evaluations:** help improve the effectiveness of training courses and other learning programs by seeking feedback from participants.

- **Embedded Quizzes:** reinforce learning as participants work their way through online learning materials.

- **Knowledge Checks:** confirm that employees have read and understood documents explaining regulations, processes, procedures, and products that they might be representing.

- **Observational Assessments:** measure skill by having a supervisor or trainer witness a person's execution of a given task.

- **Pre-course Assessments:** help direct participants to the right course and guide instructors.

- **Post-course Assessments:** determine if a candidate has the skills to perform the tasks required by the job.

- **Self-assessments:** allow new hires to reflect on their understanding and establishes a foundation for discussing their competencies, self-awareness, and their alignment with the organization's mission and values.

- **Strength Finders:** provide individuals with insights about their natural talents to help them understand and work better with others.

Compliance

Assessments are essential to a credible, defensible compliance program. They provide a means of documenting employees' knowledge of legal and regulatory requirements, as well as corporate procedures, safety rules, and equipment operation.

Assessment results must be readily available for compliance audits. For example, Know Your Customer (KYC) laws require financial institutions to verify the identity of their clients to prove the institution's compliance with anti–money laundering regulations. Employees play a crucial role in checking a client's documents to verify their identity. If financial institutions do not assess the knowledge and abilities of employees to confirm their understanding of KYC laws, they could leave themselves exposed to hefty fines for noncompliance. Similarly, healthcare organizations operate under strict regulations governing patient privacy, infection control, and other aspects of care—and face severe penalties for violating them. Regulatory compliance tests, administered within a complete compliance training program, help ensure that employees know the rules and mitigate the risk of noncompliance.

Certificate versus Certification

Certificate and certification programs differ. Certificate programs assert that someone attended and completed a course of study but not that they know or can use the behaviors or capabilities to perform related tasks. Certification programs—such as those used in IT, healthcare, education, and many other fields—recognize knowledge, skills, and professional expertise, confirming an individual's ability to perform a set of tasks. Certification programs often involve completing a study program and passing an examination. In some cases, the candidate must also have related work experience.

Licensure

A license issued by a government agency recognizes knowledge, skills, and professional expertise, confirming an individual's fitness for specific occupations and job roles. These licenses to work are commonplace for healthcare workers, such as nurses and doctors, and for professionals whose work affects public safety, such as architects, drivers, and lawyers. Licenses are regulated and often involve completing a study program and passing one or more examinations. Licenses last for a limited time and have renewal criteria such as professional development, examinations, and, in some cases, proven work experience.

Employee Satisfaction and Engagement

Measuring employees' levels of satisfaction and engagement gives organizations feedback that can prompt interventions to reduce turnover, boost productivity, and make other improvements. For decades, HR professionals have used satisfaction surveys to gauge how employees feel about everything from pay, incentives, and healthcare benefits to the work environment and opportunities for professional growth.

The Employee Net Promoter Score (eNPS) of employee satisfaction uses anonymous surveys to ask just three things:

1. How likely are employees to recommend the organization as a place to work on a 0–10 scale?

2. What do they like about the organization?

3. What do they dislike about the organization?

Scores of 9 or 10 represent promoters, 7 or 8 neutral, and 0 through 6 detractors. The resulting eNPS score is between 100 and –100: the percentage of promoters minus the percentage of detractors. This high-level survey offers a quick, easy way to take the pulse of the workforce.

In the past twenty years, efforts to boost employee engagement have come to the fore as a means of helping workers feel connected to and invested in their organizations' success. It's said that engaged employees are satisfied, but satisfied employees are not necessarily engaged. Hence the desire to nurture engaged employees, who are likely to think innovatively and go above and beyond the stated responsibilities of their jobs.

Employee satisfaction and engagement surveys are more freeform than eNPS, using write-in responses and Likert scales—which present choices, such as Strongly Agree through Strongly Disagree, to calculate levels of engagement or satisfaction. Surveys vary in length, depending on the needs of each organization.

Customer Satisfaction and Engagement

Measuring customer satisfaction helps organizations understand whether their offers and deliverables align and whether their deliverables meet customers' expectations. However, several studies in the 1990s determined that measuring satisfaction did not account for customer loyalty. Organizations are increasingly measuring customer engagement as a better indicator of loyalty and potential future purchases.

Customer satisfaction surveys come in many forms, including comment cards, online questionnaires, interviews, and colorful feedback terminals (positioned near exit doors) where departing customers can rate their experience. Net Promoter Score (NPS) uses a 0–10 scale to ask customers a single question: How likely would they be to recommend the organization's product or service to a friend or a colleague? As with the eNPS, the overall result is a score between 100 and -100. In addition to requesting a score, an NPS survey prompts the respondent to explain the reason for their score. Collating and analyzing the comments helps determine how to increase the number of promoters and reduce the number of detractors.

Customer engagement uses metrics associated with product usage and with social media consumption such as watching videos, listening to podcasts, reading blogs, adding "likes," commenting, providing reviews, and sharing content.

Today, many tools for rating customer satisfaction and engagement increasingly use Artificial Intelligence (AI). Examples of this include performing sentiment analysis on written social media posts and interpreting customers' body language and facial expressions.

As with all assessments, those related to customer satisfaction and engagement tend to produce more useful metrics when grounded with well-defined objectives and a corresponding data-collection method. It's worthwhile to define how you will measure the attribute and rate your findings against other pieces of evidence.

The Future of Assessments

Assessment technologies are advancing rapidly. We predict that, within the next few years, AI and Machine Learning (ML) will be able to create and analyze massive datasets to help drive the validity, reliability, and trustworthiness of assessments. Using performance data and examining it to determine correlation and causation will help reveal the most appropriate hiring practices, onboarding, and personal development programs. Assessments will become more trustworthy and useful.

Massive-scale automation will present some questions:

- We know that assessments can help predict future performance, but what if the future is fundamentally different from the past?

- Will the assessments we currently use help predict future performance?

- How will workers handle the ambiguity that accompanies significant change?

- Can assessments help us identify those who will be most adaptable to change?

We'll go into more detail about the future of assessment in Chapter 9. There, we will consider how exponential advances in technology will continue to change the workplace—and how assessments will keep pace.

Takeaways

- Assessments help individuals, teams, and organizations predict behaviors and performance and promote learning and change.

- Employers use assessments most commonly for recruitment, selection, promotion, onboarding, training, professional development, compliance, certification, licensure, and employee and customer engagement.

- Assessments that help determine selection, job placement, and promotion must relate to the competencies, behaviors, and capabilities required for each role.

- New types of assessments using Artificial Intelligence (AI) and Machine Learning (ML) will proliferate in the future.

5

PRINCIPLES OF MEASUREMENT

OUR DECISIONS RELATE directly to the quality of information
we can access and comprehend. A résumé, a CV, work experience, and personal interests offer valuable insights about
an individual. Interviews add worthwhile subjective evidence
of an applicant's or employee's potential. All of these sources are
worth taking into account when assessing competencies. But valid
and reliable assessments complete the picture by providing insights
that might otherwise go unnoticed. Indeed, multiple studies have
indicated that valid and reliable tests are better predictors of organization fit, job fit, and job performance than interviews.

When assessing individuals with tests, it's essential to create
high-quality instruments that measure the right things and align
with principles of measurement. When you administer an assessment, you present a stimulus, and participants respond to it. You
gather evidence from their responses, make judgments about that
evidence, then base decisions on those judgments. When you provide a high-quality stimulus, you are likely to gather high-quality
evidence from participants' answers. That evidence, in turn, leads
to informed judgments.

These principles apply whether you are testing functional skills, personality traits, preferences, values, or motives. After a functional skills assessment, you determine a score and compare it to a benchmark to potentially determine whether the candidate is qualified and able to perform a task or job.

When it comes to testing personalities, you aim to predict job fit, team fit, and behaviors rather than evaluate capabilities. As an example, you would want to know if the nursing candidate's personality makes them likely to work well under stress. You would also want to determine which work environments would or would not be suitable for them.

This chapter presents some of the principles that underlie valid, reliable, and trustworthy measurement. Our overview offers a taste of the great work done by educators, psychologists, statisticians, and others who have developed the science of measuring skills and abilities. Their achievements enable us to rely on assessment results to inform our decision-making.

Error of Measurement

We must say this right up front: All tests and surveys incorporate the principle that they have inherent inaccuracies. Error of measurement is a given. That's okay as long as the assessment's level of accuracy suits its purpose. Although you can never expect perfection from assessments, you can mitigate errors of measurement. How to do that is explained in detail shortly. Here, we discuss some standards and terminology of measurement.

Observed Score versus True Score

As much as you might like to measure the internal workings of a test taker's brain, you cannot; if you could, this would be the "true score." Many elements—everything from fatigue, anxiety, distractions, room temperature, noise, or cognitive disability to poorly written test items, lucky guesses, or cheating—can impact a test score. This "observed score" reflects evidence gained from the participant's responses to test items. If you could somehow measure every firing at every synapse within the participant's brain, you might be able to determine a "true score" of the person's actual ability. That may happen someday, but for now, you must reckon with error of measurement, which is the difference between the observed score and the true score (Figure 5.1).

Figure 5.1: Error of Measurement

How Precise Must You Be?

You don't need measurement to be perfect. You only need it to provide the information that will enable you to make a sound decision. As an example, your home scale might be off by a few ounces, but it will help you decide how much you need to eat or whether you ought to burn off some calories at the gym. It is accurate enough, but it is far from perfect. On the other hand, a technician weighing costly and volatile chemicals in a manufacturing plant would need an exact scale. Similarly, a tape measure will give you a general idea of how a couch you saw in a catalog might fit in your family room. But you'd better grab a micrometer if you need to measure the thickness of a wire.

As with physical measurements, the amount of precision you need in work-related measurement relates directly to the assessment's purpose. Skilled assessment designers aim to minimize the error of measurement by creating valid, reliable assessments that narrow the gap between the observed score and the true score.

Validity and Reliability

If you make decisions based on assessment results, your assessments must be valid and reliable. A valid assessment measures what it intends to measure, and a reliable assessment produces consistent results. Our assessments should do both!

We could write an entire book exploring validity and reliability, but others have already done so.

Please see the recommended reading list on our website at www.talenttransformation.com/book.

Dimensions of Validity and Reliability

The validity of an assessment is based on the legitimacy of the evidence collected and the conclusions drawn from the evidence. Experts have debated more than ten types of validity. For our purposes, we will discuss the five types that you are most likely to encounter:

1. **Concurrent validity** represents the agreement of conclusions reached by two different assessments. Typically, the results from a new assessment are compared to those of a well-established assessment (that has proven to be valid) to represent concurrent validity.

2. **Content validity** denotes how well a test evaluates the aspects of the subject matter it claims to measure. For example, if getting a driver's license requires passing a test, does the test adequately address topics related to the rules of the road and driving?

3. **Construct validity** is the degree to which a test measures the constructs that it claims to measure.

4. **Face validity** reflects how participants and stakeholders regard the test's "face value." For instance, do they feel that the test is trustworthy and fair? Do they have confidence in the security of the testing environment? Face validity serves to demonstrate buy-in from the respondent and is not a defensible form of validity for predicting performance.

5. **Predictive validity** signifies how well a measurement relates to future outcomes. For example, is someone who gets a high score on a driving test likely to be a safe driver?

An assessment that is valid will always be reliable. But a reliable test is not necessarily valid. To be reliable, the test must provide consistent results. Here are two ways we can view reliability:

- **Internal reliability** assesses the consistency of results across items within a test. Suppose you have a ten-question test about how to maintain and repair a 3D printer. If Subject Matter Experts (SMEs) take the test, they should get all the answers right. If they typically get one or two questions wrong, the test might be inconsistent.

- **Test-retest reliability** refers to the extent to which a measure varies from one use to another. If you give the test to SMEs five times, they should get roughly similar results each time. When an individual takes a personality test several times and sometimes emerges as an introvert and sometimes as an extrovert, you would have good reason to question the test's reliability.

Improving Validity and Reliability

Two fundamental test theories underlie the creation of valid, reliable tests. Assessment designers apply these theories to reduce error of measurement, improve an assessment's reliability, and increase the trustworthiness of its results.

Classical Test Theory (CTT)

CTT helps improve the reliability of tests by explaining the difficulty of questions and the correlation of a question's results to the overall assessment result. CTT statistics are calculated for each response and used to evaluate items and diagnose potential issues, such as a poor-performing or confusing item within the test.

CTT seeks to sort people and thus includes the concept of P-value, which represents an item's level of difficulty. P-value relates to the percentage of a cohort of candidates who responded to a question correctly. The higher the proportion of people who got it right, the easier the question is. If 80 percent of test takers answered a question correctly, its P-value would be .80. The P-value can also be calculated for incorrect choices to help determine if these distractors were credible alternatives. The P-value will vary, depending upon the cohort. If a group of novices takes the test, the P-value is likely to be lower than it would be for a group of experts.

The high-low discrimination value is also used to detect the reliability of an item within an assessment. To calculate this, you simply subtract the percentage of low-scoring respondents who answered the question correctly from the percentage of high-scoring respondents who also answered correctly. As an example, if 70 percent of high-scorers answered correctly and 25 percent of low-scoring respondents answered correctly, then the high-low discrimination is $0.70 - 0.25 = 0.45$. Another statistical property used to detect the reliability of an assessment includes a measure of internal consistency known as Cronbach's alpha.

CTT statistics can be used to set the pass/fail score to fairly divide the qualified from the not so qualified.

Item Response Theory (IRT)

IRT provides a method for comparing a test taker's underlying ability with the probability that they will answer a question correctly. So, an individual with a low ability will have a low probability of answering correctly, and someone with a high level of ability will have a high probability of answering correctly. By making these comparisons possible, IRT statistics help ensure that the test measures what it should—that it can contribute to valid test scores. As shown in Figure 5.2, IRT uses three parameters:

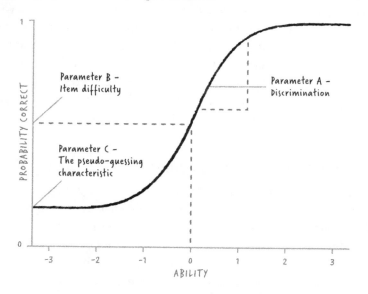

Figure 5.2: Item Response Theory (IRT) Parameters

- **Parameter A—Discrimination:** the extent to which more able test takers have a higher probability of answering the item correctly

- **Parameter B—Item difficulty:** conceptually similar to the P-value in CTT

- **Parameter C—The pseudo-guessing characteristic:** the probability that an examinee with a deficient ability level will correctly answer an item solely by guessing

IRT is more complex than CTT. But using IRT, test publishers can create fair, reliable, and Computer-Adaptive Tests (CAT) from large banks of items with various degrees of difficulty. With CAT, the selected questions are more or less difficult, depending on how well the candidate is performing. Here's how this works: If the candidate answers a question incorrectly, their next question will be slightly less challenging. If they answer the question correctly, their next question will be somewhat more difficult.

This method offers several advantages: Since you can evaluate a participant's performance using fewer questions, your tests will be shorter. Also, a test taker is unlikely to see items that are significantly below or above their level of ability. Limiting the number of questions a person sees and adapting tests to each participant's level of ability helps prevent cheating. Even if a participant shared questions with their friends, few if any of those questions would reappear.

Mitigating Errors of Measurement

Perfect measurement is unattainable, but by mitigating measurement errors, you can create assessments that achieve the right level of accuracy for each situation. You need to be more precise about some things than others, according to the nature of the job role.

When selecting someone for a highly skilled job, you don't need to know the candidate is perfect. Nor could you. You do need to know if the candidate is good enough to perform the job well. Here are some ways to achieve that.

Know What to Measure

To know what to measure, you must understand the nature of the relevant job thoroughly. A Job Task Analysis (JTA) evaluates the tasks that successful employees perform in the role. What skills does each task require? How difficult is each task? How important is it, and how often is it performed? What personal qualities make someone suitable for this job?

It's essential to match assessments to the tasks and behaviors a job requires. Suppose Dr. Smith is hiring a medical assistant. She's looking for an individual who can administer flu shots effectively yet gently—an empathetic person who won't scare patients away from returning next year. Verifying a candidate's licenses would ensure they are qualified and have the necessary job skills. But to ascertain how well the person would relate to patients, the doctor could use a formal assessment to measure their levels of empathy and observe how the candidate behaves during a role-playing exercise.

Simulate the Work Environment

The more closely an assessment comes to the actual working conditions of a job, the more accurately you can measure someone's ability to perform that job well. In a perfect world, you could test people by having them do the job they desire. However, time constraints, expense, and safety concerns might prevent that, so you need to find another option.

How might you test a would-be airline pilot? Observing them in flight would tell you a lot, but that would be way too risky, not to mention costly. The next most authentic option would be to test your aspiring pilot in a simulator. There, you could observe their performance in a safe environment to evaluate their skills before testing them in flight. Before using the simulator, you can use low-fidelity tests to confirm skills such as identifying cloud formations and flight controls, understanding safety procedures, using communication protocols, and more.

Whatever form of assessment you use, even if it's traditional, attempt to approximate what the participant will deal with at work. Let's take insurance appraisals as an example. You could write a description of a fender bender and ask the candidate questions about it, but in real life, the appraiser would look at the car to evaluate the cost of repair. Therefore, why not use a photo or videos instead of text on an insurance appraisal test? Often, a written question inadvertently checks someone's reading comprehension, distracting from the question's real purpose.

The idea of improving the fidelity of stimulus can apply to multiple-choice assessments. If you provide well-crafted stimulus and answers, a multiple-choice test can be an effective way to zero in on the information you need to glean from test results. Despite widespread resistance to multiple-choice tests, such assessments have their uses. Responses to multiple-choice questions can reflect specific aspects of an individual's skill and knowledge.

Present the Stimulus in the Appropriate Form

Alternative forms of presenting questions can make a test more engaging, but be aware of what these alternatives might require of the participant. A hot-spot or drag-and-drop question might rely on the respondent's understanding of how to interact with this response type. So, note that you might be testing a person's eyesight and motor skills when what you want to know is whether they understand the requirements of a job. Alternative question types are useful in the right circumstances but testing multiple dimensions of a person's capabilities can make it hard to ensure you measure what you intend to measure.

Set Appropriate Cut Scores

Cut scores differentiate those who are deemed capable or qualified from those who are not. On a high school pass/fail science exam, for example, a score of 70 percent or higher might indicate that the student has passed the exam. In high-stakes tests, passing an unqualified candidate could have serious consequences. One aim of this type of assessment is to set a cut score that only passes qualified candidates and not the unqualified. This requires careful analysis and due diligence. Best practices, including the use of item analysis statistics and other measures, help ensure that assessment questions are of high quality and that the cut scores you set align with what a successful person in a given role ought to achieve. A person's success on this test, together with results of psychological testing that predicts the likelihood of a good job fit, combine to help us understand a person's suitability for a given role.

If the cut score of a driving test were set incorrectly, qualified drivers might not obtain a license. Being unable to drive could impact their livelihood. Unqualified drivers who pass the test could endanger themselves and others.

Assessment Security

A test whose results will impact life, limb, or livelihood is considered a high-stakes assessment. The higher the stakes, the greater motivation there is to engage in fraud. Implementing measures to mitigate the risks of fraud is required to ensure assessments are secure. The impact on the candidate might be a better job or increased pay or injury to themselves or others. But there are also risks to organizations and society. Regulatory compliance tests help verify that employees understand their responsibilities to ensure that their organization is in compliance with laws and regulations. For example, the environment might be harmed and people injured if a worker doesn't manage toxic waste, chemicals, or pipelines effectively. Test results drive decisions made about people and the tasks that they are qualified to perform.

Each time there is a breach of test security, it reduces the trustworthiness of the test results and introduces risks. Results from high-stakes tests are essential for the health and safety of individuals, the environment, and the population in general, so these tests must be secure. Understanding and assessing threats to test security—and the potential impact of a breach—are crucial for prioritizing and developing mitigations.

Mitigate Major Forms of Fraud

Cheating is a risk when testing functional skills. As we discuss in greater detail in Chapter 6, several forms of fraud can invalidate the results of assessments:

- **Coaching:** The candidate is coached by an expert while taking the test. Ethical proctors who cannot be coerced will reduce the likelihood of coaching.

- **Copying Answers:** In this case, the candidate simply copies the answers of other test takers. Delivering a computerized test that randomly selects items and shuffles choices is one method of mitigation. Proctoring mitigates this risk for both paper and computer delivery.

- **Pre-knowledge:** The candidate receives leaked test questions in advance and can memorize the questions and answers without understanding the subject matter. Securing the test content will reduce this method of cheating.

- **Proxy Candidate:** Someone impersonates a candidate. Mitigate this risk by carefully checking the candidate's identity.

- **Results Tampering:** If the test results are not stored securely, reports are manipulated, or certificates counterfeited, the outcome of the test can be misrepresented. You can mitigate this risk by using secure systems, secure printing, and electronic credentials that you can trace to their source.

- **Using Unauthorized Aids:** Some tests are "open-book," and some are not. Open-book tests can be valid and reliable if the test taker has access to the same information while performing their tasks. However, if a candidate brings notes to reference or searches the Internet while they take a "closed" test, they are using an unauthorized aid. Proctoring is an effective way to mitigate this risk. In some cases, cameras, image analysis, and data-pattern recognition can help as well.

Use These Additional Defenses

In addition to the mitigations above, the following measures can do a lot to discourage cheating, protect the content of your tests, and detect potential problems:

- **Codes of Conduct:** Communicate an organization's expectations and create buy-in from participants. When participants know about and sign codes of conduct (also known as honor codes), they can't claim they didn't know the rules.

- **Randomization:** Draws test items from large banks so that each participant takes a unique test.

- **Secure Browsers:** Make it impossible to switch tasks or search the Internet during a computerized test.

- **Proctors:** Watch participants while they are taking tests, either on site or online.

- **High-quality Tests:** Decrease the temptation to cheat. When an organization has a reputation for providing tests that are fair and reliable, people won't be inclined to think, *This test is unfair, so it's okay for me to cheat on it.*

- **Post-test Analytics:** Post-test analytics can flag issues that merit further investigation. For example, extraordinary speed in test taking might indicate that the participant knew the answers before taking the test. When individuals select the same right and wrong answers when taking an exam at a test center, it's possible someone has coached them as a group.

The Power of Comparisons

You can establish the significance and value of a variable by comparing it to another. As an example, knowing that you scored 72 percent on a test means little unless you compare it to the passing grade or to your peers' performances.

Comparisons of assessment results indicate whether individuals or groups are qualified, learning, engaging, and performing. Here are several worthwhile types of comparison that can help you determine how you might intervene to improve learning, readiness, performance, and outcomes:

- Compare to others
- Compare to benchmark
- Compare over time (trend)
- Compare current to required level of competence
- Compare pre-event to post-event

Compare to Others

Comparing an individual's test results to a group of others occurs in a norm-referenced test. There are two ways that a test score is used in this type of test.

Comparing to a Population Norm

This comparison shows the position of the respondent within a predefined population for the trait or skill being measured. Test scores from the sample population are used for reference.

For a skills test, norm-referenced analysis determines if the respondent performed better or worse than other test takers on a skills test, but it does not indicate if the individual is qualified to perform a task.

For a personality test, a norm-referenced analysis will indicate where an individual lands on the scale being measured, compared to others in a predefined population.

Figure 5.3 can help you visualize how norm-referenced analysis provides this comparison.

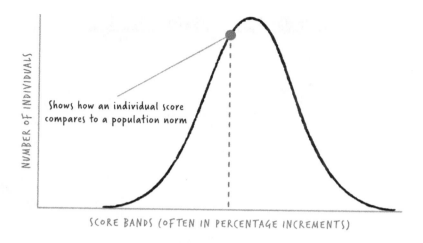

Figure 5.3: Comparison to a Population Norm

Comparing to Other Candidates

When there is a limited supply of positions open in a class or job role, you can use what is called a norm-referenced test. In this method of selection, candidates are ordered by their score, and only the top-ranking candidates will be selected.

Suppose you have only ten seats in a training class with thirty highly capable candidates who want to take the course. Lack of space means you need to choose who will get in, and you could provide a test to qualify candidates and select the top ten candidates.

Figure 5.4 can help you visualize how to compare scores from groups to derive the cut score between the candidates accepted and those who are not.

	RANK	NAME	SCORE
Accepted	1	Oretha Dorris	96.0%
	2	Jina Dobson	93.0%
	3	Jerold Passmore	90.0%
	4	Vickey Bundy	89.0%
	5	Ara Nugent	87.0%
	6	Margart Robert	85.0%
	7	Analisa Cardenas	84.0%
	8	Garret Mahaffey	83.0%
	9	Waylon Hidalgo	80.0%
	10	Ruthe Handy	79.0%
Not Accepted	11	Alex Hundley	77.0%
	12	Aide Coronado	74.0%
	13	Shaunda Kirchner	71.0%
	14	Denyse Mcneill	69.0%
	15	Rea Hopson	67.0%
	16	Tish Waugh	66.0%
	17	Yoshie Schaeffer	65.0%
	18	Kirby Ferris	63.0%
	19	Dorian Stone	61.0%
	20	Armandina Baum	58.0%
	21	Teodora Sowers	56.0%
	22	Taren Squires	54.0%
	23	Lashonda Sayre	52.0%
	24	Charity Noble	49.0%
	25	Bette Matlock	47.0%
	26	Lera Case	46.0%
	27	Gisela Moen	45.0%
	28	Harley Swartz	44.0%
	29	Rebecca Milligan	42.0%
	30	Vannesa Harlan	40.0%

Figure 5.4: Comparison to Other Candidates

Compare to Benchmark

Pass/Fail Score

Criterion-referenced tests help determine whether or not an individual is qualified to perform a task or job. When creating these types of tests, set a benchmark to separate the qualified candidates from the unqualified. For example, certification and licensing exams determine who can perform to an established standard. If you grant certification or a license to the participants with the highest scores, that's no proof that they know what they are doing. What if everyone on the test scored below 40 percent? Even the top

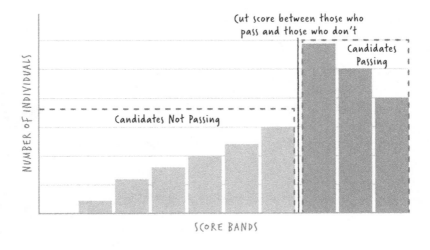

Figure 5.5: Criterion-referenced Cut Score

scorers would be unfit. For criterion-referenced tests to be valid and reliable, you need to analyze the required tasks and the skills necessary to perform those tasks, then set mastery levels for the task based on statistics (see Figure 5.5).

We can calculate cut scores using these methods:

- **Informed judgment** (usable but not recommended), whereby an SME specifies criteria (number of correct answers, number of attempts, cut score percentage, and so forth).

- **Borderline group**, which involves SMEs interviewing participants or making professional judgments of a cut score before a test to identify those whose likeliness of passing or failing the test is in doubt. Maybe they will pass the test and perhaps they won't. After the test, the scores of these borderline individuals achieve help determine the cut score.

- **The Angoff Method**, which involves polling SMEs in a workshop setting. The SMEs consider the probability that a marginal individual would get specific questions right (0–100 percent). They then exclude or modify problematic items and use a mathematical calculation to set the cut score.

- **Contrasting group**, which compares the test scores of competent performers and a suitable group of non-competent individuals to narrow the range of the cut score. Set the cut score to avoid qualifying novices or disqualifying experts. Figure 5.6 can help you visualize how to compare scores from groups to derive a cut score.

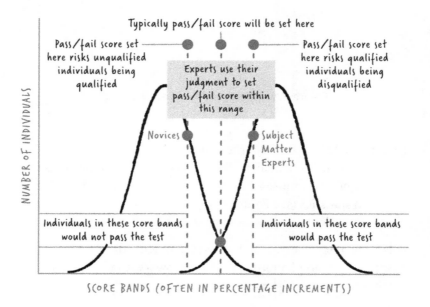

Figure 5.6: Comparing Groups

Industry/Organization/Population Norm as a Benchmark

You can establish norms for Key Performance Indicators (KPIs) such as financial metrics, performance metrics, and customer satisfaction, as well as assessments of personality traits, values, preferences, behavioral styles, and functional skills. You can use internal or external data to establish norms for such indicators. As an example, when your high-performing salespeople take a personality assessment, the resulting data can help set norms for hiring or promoting individuals into that position. Alternatively, you could make judgments based on a test publisher's established norms for high-performing salespeople.

Compare over Time (Trend)

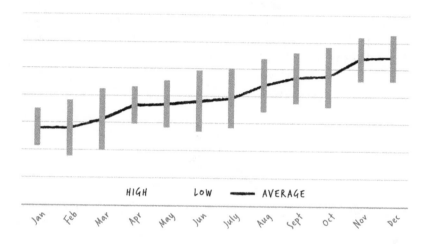

Figure 5.7: Trends over Time

Trend analysis—plotting data against time and then interpreting the trend graph (see Figure 5.7)—can help you identify problems within an organization, such as reduced employee engagement or customer satisfaction. You can also use trend analysis to track test content leakage when test scores are improving because candidates are sharing examination content. For example, if you notice that more people are passing a test each week, you might discover that participants are sharing the questions, and their friends are cheating. (This is the pre-knowledge form of fraud discussed earlier.)

Falling scores, on the other hand, might point to a different type of problem—perhaps an instructor is missing the mark.

Compare Current to Required Level of Competence

The changing nature of work calls for new tasks and skills. To navigate from the current state to the future state will require clarity and planning. Identifying the skills gaps at the individual, team, or organization level allows for orderly knowledge transfer and skills development. Using assessments to track these gaps over time makes it easier to confirm that you're on target to have the right skills in place when you need them. Figure 5.8 provides a spider chart that can help identify skills gaps.

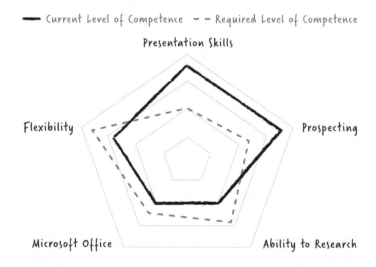

Figure 5.8: Comparing Levels of Competence

Compare Pre-event to Post-event

Measuring something before and after an event helps us determine whether or not an intervention worked. For example, increased sales after the introduction of a new process, product, or service

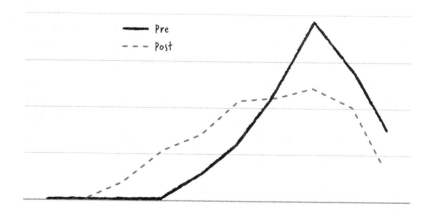

Figure 5.9: Comparing Pre-event to Post-event Test Scores

could be a measure of sales and marketing effort or customer acceptance. Another example would be tests used before and after a course to detect if any knowledge transfer occurred during the learning experience. Figure 5.9 shows how a comparison might be represented for pre- and post-event test scores.

Correlation versus Causation

Data and graphics provide valuable insights but cannot necessarily lead you to the interventions that may be required to achieve your objectives. Having delivered valid, reliable assessments and used the results to make worthwhile comparisons, you can spot correlations and dig deeper to identify causation. Correlation and causation are familiar but little-understood terms. You probably have heard that "correlation does not imply causation." When there is a correlation, it's essential to understand whether you have identified the cause or if there is simply a coincidence.

Discovering a correlation between pre-employment test results, onboarding experiences, employee engagement, certifications, satisfaction surveys, and organizational performance is useful. Determining which factors are supporting performance is even better.

Correlation takes the form of a number that describes the direction and size of the relationship between two or more variables. Two or more variables are said to be correlated if an increase or decrease in the value of one coincides with a change in the other's value. The variables would be correlated even if the change is in the opposite direction.

Let's consider these two variables: income and work hours. Jane earns an hourly rate. As Jane's work hours increase, she makes more money. You can safely say that these variables are correlated. Let's also look at product prices and buying power. As prices rise, Jack's purchasing power decreases. He cannot afford those products anymore. So, product prices and buying power are indeed correlated, but inversely.

Although two variables change in relation to each other, the change in one does not necessarily cause the other. For example, you might notice an increase in the number of lost bags in airport terminals when attendance at college basketball games spikes. These two events correlate, but did one cause the other? Probably not.

Another, now famous, correlation connected the decreasing tonnage of fresh lemons imported from Mexico to the United States with the declining number of highway fatalities on U.S. highways between 1996 and 2000. Common sense would reject most explanations of this correlation and conclude that this was pure coincidence.

Causation is in play only when one event or change directly causes another change or event, rather than just coinciding with it. For example, you know that taking a particular antibiotic cures a specific infection, or that driving while drowsy increases the risk of motor vehicle accidents. However, sometimes distinguishing between correlation and direct causation isn't easy. For example, if a study found that people who eat two cups of spinach a day have a reduced risk for heart disease, it would not necessarily be correct to conclude that eating spinach prevents heart disease. People who consume plenty of spinach might also be more likely to engage in healthy eating, regular exercise, etc. Researchers would have to control for these factors before drawing any conclusions about their findings.

Why Differentiate between Causation and Correlation?

Although identifying the correct relationship between events isn't easy, it's crucial. As indicated in the previous example, mistaking correlation for causation can lead us to incorrect conclusions. That's why scientists and statisticians continually conduct research to determine correlation, causation, and the degree to which they apply to variables in a variety of fields, from medicine to economics. Consider these questions:

- Does the incidence of on-the-job injuries decline when utility workers receive training?

- Does advertising a product increase revenue?

- Does taking a specific drug relieve a particular type of pain?

- Does a vegan diet lead to a longer and healthier life?

- Does education level impact a person's health?

- Do fuel consumption and a modern lifestyle influence climate change?

You can't answer these questions without first identifying a correlation between the variables in them. Then you can determine if the relationship is causal or not.

Determining Causation

Using randomized controlled studies is the most effective way to establish causality between variables. The more information you gather through these studies, the easier it will be to understand whether one event causes the other or if the two events are merely related—even coincidental. It would be unethical for researchers to subject a group of people to harmful conditions intentionally, so controlled studies have their limitations.

In a randomized controlled study, participants are divided randomly into two groups as identical to each other as possible. The variable in question is changed for one group of participants, but not the other, to see if that change affects the outcome. A classic example of this, from the medical field, is a placebo-controlled study in which one group with a disease-related sign or symptom receives a placebo (a substance that appears to be a drug but has no active ingredient) and the other gets an experimental drug. If the number of participants who experience a positive change in the sign or symptom is significantly higher among those who receive the drug as opposed to the placebo, then the study suggests—but does not prove—that the drug caused the change. Accumulating evidence of causality from multiple studies is essential to support the validity of the proposed causation.

Takeaways

- Valid, reliable assessments are powerful predictors of team fit, job fit, and job performance.

- No assessment is perfect, but an assessment's level of accuracy must suit its purpose.

- Skillful design minimizes error of measurement and increases test validity and reliability.

- Effective defenses are required to guard against fraud to protect test validity.

- Comparisons help us understand the meaning of assessment results.

- Establishing causation, not just correlation, leads to the most appropriate intervention.

ASSESSING
INDIVIDUALS

INDIVIDUALS' BEHAVIORS and capabilities underpin the work of teams and organizations. Assessing people's competencies plays an essential role in recruiting, learning, coaching, promotion, and certification. The intent is to evaluate each person fairly and accurately, so that they end up in a suitable job, positioned to perform effectively and progress further.

In this chapter, we examine the use of assessments to measure an individual's personality, behaviors, knowledge, skills, and capabilities against the competencies their current or desired job requires. We also explore how assessments can predict the likelihood of a person's success in a new role—a valuable tool for identifying individuals best suited for roles that will emerge in the coming years.

For Effective Assessments, Start with Competencies

Competencies appear near the top of the Talent Transformation Pyramid (p. 47) in Chapter 3. Competency definitions provide valuable information for developing job descriptions, learning experiences, and effective assessments. They document the knowledge, skills, and behaviors that individuals or teams require to perform a task, describe performance conditions, and include criteria for potential levels of performance.

Competency Models

Organizations group individual competency definitions into competency models (also known as competency frameworks) that explain the required behaviors and capabilities of a job. Competency definitions also describe the required performance environment—the physical setting in which an individual or team performs a task, including elements such as information, job aids, tools, workspace, air quality, noise level, and lighting—and the levels of potential performance. These models explain what's needed to perform successfully in a role; they help us understand what we need to measure to determine if someone is suitable for that role.

A model that incorporates all the competencies and levels of competence required of a role informs

- job descriptions;
- assessments for selecting candidates for a job;
- assessments of an employee's performance; and
- employee training and development.

Figure 6.1 illustrates the relationship between a competency definition and its components within a competency model.

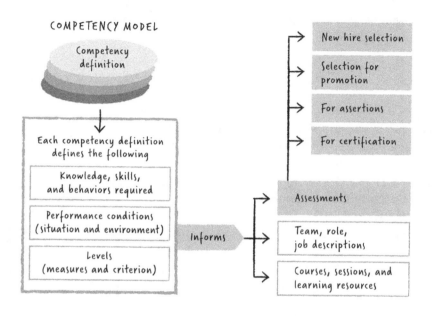

Figure 6.1: Competency Model and Definitions

In creating such a model, we can use Job Task Analysis (JTA) to tease out critical tasks and discover their importance, difficulty, and frequency. For existing roles, we analyze each task by surveying and interviewing the individuals—preferably experts—who already perform them. For a new or changing role, Subject Matter Experts (SMEs) collaborate to determine the details of the tasks it will entail.

Competency models specify the levels of performance a job requires. For instance, an accountant might need highly advanced Excel skills, while a sales manager could probably function well with intermediate skills.

In the future, with the support of new technologies, such as natural language processing, competency models will become easier to maintain and more useful. We discuss these exciting developments in Chapter 9.

Defining Competencies

To create fair, trustworthy assessments, you must start with well-defined competencies that detail the measurable patterns of behaviors and capabilities—including the knowledge, skills, and other characteristics—that an individual needs to perform the tasks of a role.

Competency definitions document the following elements:

- Behaviors and capabilities a task requires

- Benchmarks for measuring the level of competency

- Conditions in which an individual will have to perform

- Learning and development opportunities for individuals who don't achieve the benchmarks

Figure 6.2 illustrates how competency definitions incorporate the Talent Transformation Pyramid's factors and relate to job roles.

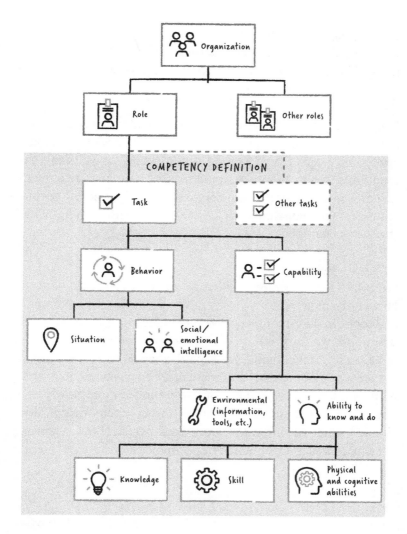

Figure 6.2: Competency Definition Relationships

These definitions guide us in assessing and measuring performance. They also delineate differentiating levels such as "needs improvement or support," "meets expectation," and "exceeds expectation."

Two Types of Competencies

Competency definitions that relate to behavior and those that relate to capabilities require different approaches. One size does not fit all.

Behavioral

Behaviors are situation-dependent, so we need to understand a role and its requirements before we can define the behaviors it demands. For instance, a worker in a healthcare organization who deals with emotional family members would need to demonstrate empathy. A janitor working for the same organization might need to demonstrate tact when dealing with individuals who leave things where they don't belong.

Capability-Related

Capability-related competencies represent what an individual should know or be able to do on the job, given the necessary information and tools. In describing required capabilities within a competency definition, we must identify the tools and information that will enhance or limit an individual's performance. As an example, an author who can research and write daily blog articles on a laptop with an Internet connection would work much more slowly using books and a typewriter. Therefore, the competency definition should include the information and tools available for performing the task as well as the required performance metrics.

Organizations typically document about four to fifteen behavioral competencies. In contrast, they might document hundreds of capability competencies. The more heavily regulated the industry, the more rigorous the documentation process for defining the capabilities required to perform the tasks.

Why Assess Individuals?

In Chapter 4, we described assessments as potent predictors of readiness and performance. Valid and reliable assessments should predict how well, and how safely, someone will perform the tasks of their role. Yes, we often test learners after they have undergone training, but the underlying reason for doing this is to determine whether or not they're ready to perform the tasks the job requires. Assessments do help us predict future performance, particularly if we can create a test environment that simulates the work environment. The closer the assessment stimulus matches what happens on the job, the more likely the assessment will predict an individual's potential to perform.

Organizations use assessments to predict readiness based on behavioral and capability-related competencies. Let's look at both of these categories.

To Predict Behaviors

Several factors influence on-the-job behaviors, including the following:

- Personality traits, such as openness, neuroticism, extraversion, conscientiousness, humility, and agreeableness

- Values, beliefs, and preferences

- The learning experiences that help people develop social and emotional intelligence

- An individual's current situation

Understanding an individual's values, motives, preferences, and personality traits provides clues about what type of organization, job role, and situation would suit them. Yet individuals might struggle to represent themselves effectively if asked directly about their typical behaviors, personality, preferences, beliefs, or values. Carefully crafted assessments can tease these out with insightful questions developed to uncover the patterns in the answers they provide. Assessments of personality, for example, can help identify the kinds of misalignment that commonly frustrate people at work. Consider the following examples:

- Someone who values altruism works for a company that cares more about commercial success than good citizenship.

- An extrovert who draws strength from communicating with others works in isolation with few personal interactions.

- The employer of an individual who focuses on getting results insists that they strictly follow a process.

There is never a perfect fit, just as there is never an ideal organization, but the closer the fit, the less stress the individual will experience on the job. Stress, generated by internal conflict or by a difficult situation, might trigger negative behaviors. You can use assessments to predict negative behaviors when someone is under pressure. As an example, an individual who is perceptive and insightful might overuse these traits when under stress and become critical of others, cynical, and distrustful.

Even when someone is already in a role—and it's fairly clear how well the job suits them—assessments can help enhance performance in a variety of ways. For instance, feedback from 180-degree and 360-degree assessments—which compare an individual's ratings of their performance with ratings they receive from their colleagues—makes the individual more aware of how others perceive them (see Figure 6.3). Realizing how coworkers see them can encourage the person to develop new social and emotional skills and improve their levels of engagement, satisfaction, and performance. Receiving this feedback provides an opportunity for reflection and growth, helping the individual determine what kind of learning and coaching would help them grow and progress.

Dan, a customer service manager, was quite happy with his 360-degree assessment. He had received high marks for his overall performance. The hires he'd trained were performing well, and customer satisfaction was high. But one result rankled him: A few colleagues mentioned that he was sometimes too lenient with the handful of workers who weren't pulling their weight. After reflecting on this feedback, Dan discussed the issue with his boss. She shared some experiences of her own and referred him to a website that offered pointers on effective management. Dan began paying closer attention to what was happening among team members, detecting problems, and resolving them quickly.

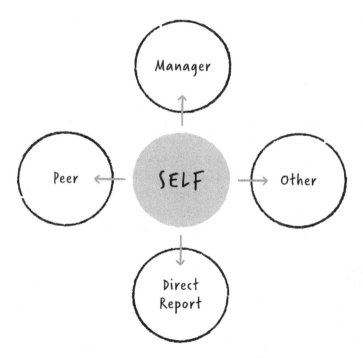

Figure 6.3: Participants in a 360-degree Assessment

For descriptions of these and many other types of assessments, see the table in Appendix B and on the website at www.talenttransformation.com/book.

To Predict Capabilities

As noted earlier, before you can predict an individual's capabilities, you need to understand the knowledge, skills, and abilities required to perform their tasks and the tools and information they will use. Once that's understood, testing technical and functional skills will help you predict whether someone will be able to perform in a job. However, skills tests won't tell the whole story. Predicting capabilities requires a holistic approach that includes considering how an individual will respond to a particular work environment.

Morgan aced the welding skills test she took when applying for a job in a precision machine shop. She performed well in the controlled testing environment and demonstrated that she had excellent technical and functional skills. But how will she do in a busy shop that's about to start a huge project? Joe, the foreman, knows enough about the work to anticipate the pressure. He'd like to figure out how this recruit is likely to cope with such a heavy workload. HR asked Morgan how she has handled stressful situations and how she expects to deal with a heavy workload. Morgan assured HR that she is ready for this challenge. Joe, now reasonably confident that Morgan will perform well, asks her to start work next week. Until Joe observes Morgan on the job, using the same tools and information as her coworkers, he won't know for sure how successful she will be. But her skills test results and her reassuring answers to interview questions make it highly likely she will rise to the challenge.

When to Assess Individuals

Assessment plays a valuable role at every stage of employment, from recruitment onwards.

Recruitment

Pre-employment assessments come into play at various stages in the talent acquisition process. When recruiters have a glut of applicants, readily available assessments can screen out unsuitable candidates early in the process. These can be as simple as self-assessments that help candidates understand whether they have the skills required for the role. In contrast, when there is a shortage of applicants, recruiters can use assessments to entice candidates into the recruitment pipeline. For example, they can offer these assessments on social media to help prospective candidates understand if their skills match the role and start seeding the idea of changing employers.

Once candidates qualify for consideration, pre-employment assessments can help determine job fit and whether the candidate has the functional skills required. These assessments, along with interviews and background checks, provide crucial information to determine if a candidate will perform well on the job. You can use off-the-shelf tests—validated for the open role—to assess personality, behavioral style, emotional intelligence, and functional skills. Some organizations with sizable hiring needs for a specific job role might instead develop assessments themselves and take on the responsibility of ensuring that the test is reliable and properly validated.

Onboarding

As someone new joins an organization, they typically need to acquire both organization-specific and generic skills. These areas of learning call for different approaches to assessment. New hires must learn insider information about the organization's policies, processes, tools, job aids, culture, benefits, and so forth. When these topics are organization-specific, you should develop and validate assessment instruments to test the new employees' knowledge and skills. Depending on the role, test results might qualify or disqualify an individual for continued employment in that role. High-stakes tests present higher consequences to the individual or organization, so build and analyze these tests with great care.

Testing new hires' acquisition of generic skills, such as using email software and managing their time, is more straightforward. Validated off-the-shelf assessments offer cost-effective solutions for testing new hires after they complete in-house training, e-learning, or college courses, for instance.

Professional Development

As an individual develops on-the-job skills, they increase their value to the organization—and they raise it higher by endeavoring to learn more. In the new world of work, tasks might change even if the job title remains the same, and employees will move to new jobs more regularly than before. In short, the changing nature of work is likely to follow this cycle: learn, apply that learning to tasks, then change roles and get a new set of tasks. This learn/work/change pattern (Figure 6.4) will repeat itself as automation replaces tasks previously performed by humans. Notice the vital role that lifelong learning will play in helping individuals to keep developing new functional, social, and emotional intelligence skills.

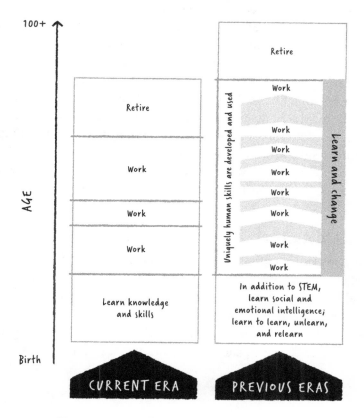

Figure 6.4: The Learn/Work/Change Pattern

Given this ongoing demand for professional development, employees will need assessments that can help them understand and improve their

- behavioral styles by showing how their current styles might be working or not, and providing opportunities to reflect; and

- functional skills by highlighting what gaps they need to fill to perform better in their current job role or to qualify for a new job.

In both cases, unless skilled professionals provide coaching, employees can misinterpret assessment results that could negatively impact them, their team, or the organization. Some people might only focus on positive feedback and ignore the negative, or vice versa.

Imagine Bill, a sales manager, whose 360-degree assessment rated him high for leading his team when they achieved record sales but low when it came to an unacceptable level of employee turnover. Bill might be so delighted with his rating for excellent sales that he overlooks the problem with retention and never bothers to identify a solution. A professional experienced in the art of interpreting results would tease out the subtleties of Bill's situation, help him recognize his shortcomings, and guide him into learning experiences that will help him improve how he relates to his colleagues.

What to Assess

Assessments of individuals cover a wide array of topics—anything and everything related to an individual's skills, abilities, and behavioral style. Taking self-assessments that identify personal strengths helps individuals navigate career paths that make the most of their best attributes. Here is a sampling of the many issues that surveys, quizzes, tests, exams, and other forms of assessment address.

See Appendix B for an extensive list of assessments and their uses and a more comprehensive list on the website at www.talenttrans formation.com/book.

Physical Abilities

Tests of physical ability typically ask individuals to perform job-related tasks requiring manual labor or physical skill. These tasks require physical abilities, such as strength, flexibility, and stamina.

Examples of Physical Ability Tests

- **Muscular Tension Tests:** Tasks requiring pushing, pulling, and lifting

- **Muscular Power Tests:** Tasks requiring the individual to overcome some initial resistance (e.g., loosening a nut on a bolt)

- **Muscular Endurance Tests:** Tasks involving repetitions of tool use (e.g., removing objects from belts)

- **Cardiovascular Endurance Tests:** Tasks assessing aerobic capacity (e.g., climbing stairs)

- **Flexibility Tests:** Tasks that involve bending, twisting, stretching, or reaching of a body segment (e.g., installing lighting fixtures)

- **Balance Tests:** Tasks in which stability of body position is hard to maintain (e.g., standing on rungs of a ladder)

While some physical ability tests may require electronically monitored machines, equipment needs can often be kept simple. For example, stamina can be measured with a treadmill and an electrocardiograph, or with a challenging hike. However, a possible drawback of using such straightforward methods is imprecise measurement.

Organizations should consider the following issues when using physical ability tests:

- Employment selection based on physical abilities can be litigious. Legal challenges have arisen because physical ability tests—especially those involving strength and endurance—tend to screen out a disproportionate number of women and some ethnic minorities. Therefore, it is crucial to have validity evidence justifying the job-relatedness of physical ability measures.

- Candidates could injure themselves while performing physical ability tests. For example, a test involving heavy lifting could result in a back injury or aggravate an existing medical condition. Jobs such as firefighting are hazardous by nature, so firefighters' physical tests of ability might subject them to potential hazards. With safety in mind, you can simulate some scenarios, but not all.

- Many countries regulate physical ability tests that involve monitoring heart rate, blood pressure, or other physiological factors. Some jurisdictions categorize these as medical exams and prohibit administering them before offering a job. The job offer will be contingent on the exam results.

Cognitive Abilities

Cognitive abilities are mental skills that enable us to carry out tasks. These core thought-based abilities enable us to learn, listen, remember, solve problems, and pay attention:

- **Sustained Attention:** The fundamental ability to look at, listen to, and think about tasks over time. Learning depends on it. Learning, comprehending, and committing new facts to memory cannot happen without sustained attention.

- **Response Inhibition:** The ability to constrain one's response to distractions. Imagine two people who hear the "ping" of an incoming message on their phones. The person who maintains attention has better response inhibition.

- **Speed of Information Processing:** How quickly an individual can process incoming information. Speed of information processing is a central aspect of IQ (intelligence quotient).

- **Cognitive Flexibility:** An individual's ability to shift their thinking to adapt to new stimuli—to change their perspective as they change what they are thinking about, how they are thinking about it, and what they think about it. Cognitive flexibility is a crucial skill for research and working in teams.

- **Multiple Simultaneous Attention:** The ability to shift one's attention and effort back and forth between two or more simultaneous activities. This ability makes demands on sustained attention, response inhibition, and information-processing speed.

- **Working Memory:** The ability to remember instructions or keep information in mind long enough to perform tasks. We use working memory when we look at a phone number and keep it in mind while we dial it. Working memory is the mental sketch pad where we put things to think about and manipulate.

- **Category Formation:** The ability to organize information, concepts, and skills into categories. It is the cognitive basis for higher-level abilities such as applying, analyzing, and evaluating those concepts and skills.

- **Pattern Recognition and Inductive Thinking:** A unique ability of the human brain not only to find patterns but also to figure out logically what those patterns might predict. In a broad sense, pattern recognition and inductive thinking form the basis for all scientific inquiry.

IQ tests are problematic if used for recruiting or promotion, as they are poor predictors of job performance and tend to discriminate against minorities and protected groups. IQ test results provide a score that rates the subject compared to the general population—an estimate of their intelligence. However, these scores might include errors of measurement caused by the need to understand English and cultural trivia.

Cognitive aptitude tests are used for pre-employment testing to measure someone's general ability to solve problems and understand concepts. Defensible and valid cognitive aptitude tests must align with the requirements of the job and measure such things as reasoning ability, problem-solving ability, capacity to perceive relationships between things, and ability to store and retrieve information. The tests may also measure the following:

- **Spatial Awareness:** The ability to visualize manipulation of shapes.

- **Mathematical Ability:** The ability to solve mathematical problems and use logic.

- **Language Ability:** Sometimes including the ability to complete sentences or recognize words rearranged or missing letters.

- **Memory Ability:** The ability to recall things presented either visually or aurally.

- **Problem-solving Ability:** The ability to solve abstract problems.

- **Critical Thinking:** The ability to digest and apply information, learn new skills, and think critically.

Cognitive aptitude tests generally measure an individual's aptitude. Individuals with high aptitude are more likely to be quick learners and high performers than are individuals with low aptitude.

Personality

Personality tests systematically elicit information about a person's motivations, values, preferences, interests, emotional makeup, and style of interacting with people and situations. The results of personality assessments can help you evaluate an individual's potential fit with a job role or team. These tests most commonly consist of self-report inventories (questionnaires) that ask applicants to rate their level of agreement with statements designed to evaluate their personality traits. Profiles based on these self-assessments identify personal preferences and help predict job fit, team fit, and satisfaction.

Personality Trait Theory

Personality trait theory provides models that help explain the relationship between personality and behaviors. These models represent a personality trait, or sub-trait, as a quotient on a scale, not as right or wrong, on or off. An individual's personality combines many traits and sub-traits, and it is unwise to use a single trait to predict behaviors on the job. For example, people of high integrity may follow the rules and be easy to supervise. But if they are not outgoing, patient, and friendly, they are unlikely to provide high-quality customer service.

Traits, sub-traits, or combinations that predict performance vary according to the role in question. When selecting or developing a personality test, it makes sense to start with discovering which traits will help someone be successful in the position. It is common practice to assess individuals who are successful in a specific job role and use the results as benchmarks for potential success. However, this practice does not always yield an accurate representation of what is truly driving these individuals' success.

Hundreds of personality traits have been identified and grouped in various ways. For example, several sets of independent researchers measured numerous personality traits and sub-traits. They used the statistical technique of factor analysis to group them into the Big Five, known as OCEAN or CANOE. More recently, another team added honesty-humility to designate the Big Six, also called HEXACO.

OCEAN	CANOE	HEXACO
Openness to experience	Conscientiousness	Honesty-humility
Conscientiousness	Agreeableness	Emotionality
Extraversion	Neuroticism	eXtraversion
Agreeableness	Openness to experience	Agreeableness
Neuroticism	Extraversion	Conscientiousness
		Openness to experience

The only differences between these models is that HEXACO uses the word "Emotionality" instead of "Neuroticism" and includes "Honesty-humility" as a significant trait.

Psychologist Raymond Cattell developed a grouping structure known as the Sixteen Personality Factor Model (16PF). Figure 6.5 displays an individual's quotients of each personality factor:

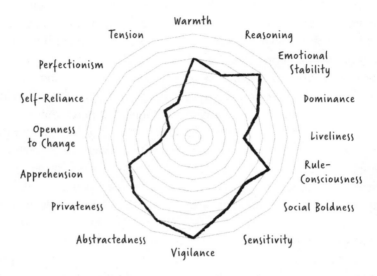

Figure 6.5: Spider Graph of an Individual's
Sixteen Personality Factor (16PF) Profile

Assessing personality traits for selection and promotion includes administering a questionnaire to an individual and comparing their results to norms deemed appropriate for a specific job role. However, you can also use results from these questionnaires for career, team, and management development.

On-the-Job Behavior

An individual's behavior will vary with the stresses and strains of their job. To determine how they might behave in each circumstance, you might use interviews, observations, or timed exercises to simulate a realistic situation and see how the person performs. Activities might include assigning an "in-basket" of emails, telephone calls, or documents, and having the person set priorities, organize their work schedule, and respond appropriately to the inbox items.

Psychiatric Diagnosis

Some personality tests help diagnose mental illnesses (e.g., paranoia, schizophrenia, obsessive-compulsive disorders, and so on), rather than work-related personality traits. Airline pilots and public safety professionals are examples of individuals who might undergo psychiatric evaluations before they are allowed to start work. Many jurisdictions consider any test designed to reveal such psychiatric disorders as a "medical examination." A qualified medical professional must administer the test only after the employer offers the candidate a job, which will be contingent on the medical report.

Emotional Intelligence

Recall from Chapter 3 that emotional intelligence is a type of social competence involving the ability to monitor one's own and others' emotions, to discriminate among them, and to use the information to guide one's thinking and actions. Emotional intelligence connects a person's cognitive processes to their emotional processes.

Skills and abilities related to emotional intelligence have five domains:

1. **Self-awareness:** Observing oneself and recognizing a feeling as it happens.

2. **Emotion Management:** Consciously managing emotions by realizing what is behind a feeling and finding ways to handle fears and anxieties, anger, and sadness.

3. **Self-motivation:** Channeling emotions in the service of a goal; emotional self-control, delaying gratification, and stifling impulses.

4. **Empathy:** Being sensitive to others' feelings and concerns, taking their perspective, and appreciating the differences in how people feel about things.

5. **Handling Relationships:** Understanding others' emotions, thereby communicating with social competence and using social skills to form constructive relationships.

Measuring emotional intelligence typically involves asking scenario-based questions of candidates and scoring their responses based on expert judgment (expert scoring) or consensus among a large number of people (consensus scoring). For example, candidates taking an emotional intelligence test view a series of faces and identify which emotions they detect. Their answers provide insights into how the individual can perceive emotions in others. In another emotional intelligence assessment, candidates answer questions about how they would understand and communicate with an anxious, stressed, discouraged, or grieving employee.

Strengths

When people recognize their strengths and focus on them, they are more productive and engaged. They perform better and take greater joy in work and life. So, it's not surprising that people take strength-finder assessments to identify the combination of skills, talents, knowledge, and experience that make them unique. Sometimes these strengths are apparent, but such a self-assessment can reveal attributes that might otherwise go unnoticed. When people understand their strengths, they are likely to channel their energies into successful endeavors and chart clearer career paths. Words such as adaptable, analytical, competitive, consistent, deliberate, empathetic, futuristic, responsible, and positive are typically used to describe strengths.

Organizations use strength-finder assessments to help employees appreciate their strengths and direct them to potential career paths. Unlike personality tests, these types of assessments require little expert interpretation, so individuals often buy them for their personal use.

More advanced strength-finder assessments explain a participant's strengths in detail and suggest how to apply them to their personal life or career. These assessments display the person's strengths in rank order and often explain the potential downsides of these strengths. For instance, an empathetic person is likely to connect well with others, but deep empathy could put the person at risk of being manipulated. Making participants aware of these pit-falls helps them know what to look for and how to mitigate potential problems.

Functional Skills

Functional skills tests are also known as summative tests, job knowl-edge tests, achievement tests, or mastery tests. They are used to evaluate technical or professional expertise in a specific domain. These types of tests are based on an analysis of the tasks that make up the job. They are useful for recruitment, after training events, and for certifications.

Unlike cognitive ability tests, skills tests don't assess learning potential. They can tell employers what an individual currently knows, but not whether they can rely on the individual to master new material quickly.

Here are some situations that call for functional skills tests:

- Screening applicants who must possess skills before being hired

- Placing individuals in jobs that require specialized or technical knowledge

- Assessing candidates' knowledge of topics such as basic account-ing principles, computer programming, financial management, and knowledge of contract law

- Post-recruitment training/onboarding

- Post-training, to ensure that an individual is qualified to take on a role, especially when health, safety, and regulatory compliance are part of the person's responsibilities

- Identifying knowledge and skills gaps to help direct or focus learning

- Providing memory retrieval practice and skills development

- Licensing and professional certification

Experience

Assessing someone's experience can help you predict their future performance. As an example, it's fair to conclude that a manager's success leading teams in the past would indicate that they could lead teams in the future in a similar context. Experience counts! To ensure a fair and reliable selection process, systematically evaluate a candidate's experience—including academic achievements, employment history, and other endeavors.

You can usually evaluate experiences early in the selection process to identify applicants who meet the minimum requirements. To determine how an experience might affect job performance, focus on the competencies you have identified through a job analysis. Suppose you are looking for someone to work in Information Technology (IT) and collaborate with your Beijing office. If an applicant has been studying Chinese and Machine Learning (ML) in China, your eyes light up. You figure that this person could have the capabilities this job requires. But you need more to go on than your hunch.

Thanks to records from schools, colleges, and universities, it won't be hard to evaluate the candidate's academic experience. But what about their career to date? The applicant worked a few years before going abroad, so you will want to find out how well they performed in their previous jobs.

It's not always easy to get accurate, consistent records of employee experiences, but try to learn as much as you can. Sometimes an HR system will record an individual's experiences, but future employers might not have access to such records. You can ask the candidate about their previous experiences, but you will need to double-check what they say by cross-referencing them via social media or former colleagues.

When rating previous on-the-job experiences, you can look at the amount and quality of the applicant's experience. Judgments tend to be subjective, but those familiar with the tasks the individual will need to perform can help develop the criteria and benchmarks. In addition to work, you can use other relevant experiences—such as community service volunteering—to inform judgments.

One method for systematically assessing a candidate's experience is to present a task statement and ask whether they have ever performed the task and, if so, what they regard as their level of proficiency when performing it. The more tasks the candidate has accomplished, and the higher their levels of skill, the higher the candidate's score.

As with most self-reported instruments, candidate inflation or distortion can threaten the validity of this style of assessment. Two ways to combat these risks are to:

1. Create an expectation that the candidate's responses will be verified.

2. Carry out verification procedures and adjust scores based on the findings.

Where to Assess

The proliferation of devices connected to the Internet has dramatically increased the number and availability of assessments. The traditional testing center is now just one of many places to deliver tests.

Work, School, Home, Just About Any Place

Today, it is easy to take surveys, quizzes, tests, and exams anywhere in the world and on a variety of devices. Remote testing has many advantages. For example, being able to access pre-employment screening tests from home, a college campus, or a café saves candidates time and travel costs. For employers, flexible delivery options widen the pool of potential applicants.

Whether you administer assessments in classrooms, testing centers, or at kitchen tables, you must provide security that matches the stakes and style of the assessment. Traditional testing venues have built-in ways to protect assessment security. But even when testing remotely, you can prevent or mitigate these three types of fraud discussed in Chapter 5:

1. Identity fraud, which occurs when a proxy candidate takes the test on behalf of the candidate. Reducing this threat includes dual-factor authentication, checking government-issued identity documents, reviewing patterns of data over time, and using online proctors. The proctor would ask the participant to answer random questions about their background, have them scan the room with a camera to ensure there are no inappropriate resources available there, and watch them take the test.

2. Using unauthorized information from sources such as Wikipedia or Google to search for answers. Ways to mitigate this risk include using online proctors, locking down the technology, and checking data after the event.

3. Pre-knowledge of assessment items, which allows a candidate to learn the answers ahead of time. When test-preparation providers and e-commerce stores sell stolen items from previous tests, they tip the balance in favor of their customers. Using randomized items from large question banks can protect against this, as can creating fresh assessment content.

Cheating is less of an issue with personality assessments. After all, even if someone received coaching ahead of time, it would be difficult to fake out such a test. Even if someone could do that, how likely would they be to land a job that they would enjoy?

Assessment Centers

Assessment centers administer a wide array of assessments to help identify the most promising candidates for selection, career development, promotion, and other employment decisions. Some organizations use assessment centers to evaluate managerial and leadership skills. These assessments include everything from proctored exams, psychometric tests, and interviews to group discussions and exercises to evaluate candidates' personalities and aptitudes.

The benefits of conducting assessments in the controlled environment of an assessment center include greater security for the employer, higher reliability and consistency of assessment results, and greater fairness for candidates.

Many assessment-center exercises simulate on-the-job challenges. These activities help organizations evaluate job-related competencies, including functional skills, interpersonal skills, oral and written communication, planning and evaluating, and reasoning and problem-solving. Role-playing, for example, might call on an applicant to demonstrate how they would handle an angry customer, to determine how well the applicant listens to the customer, confirms their understanding, displays empathy, de-escalates the situation, and resolves the problem.

By measuring a broad range of knowledge, skills, and abilities and observing on-the-job behaviors, assessment centers take a holistic approach to predicting a candidate's likelihood of success in a particular job.

Takeaways

- Successful assessments are based on well-defined competencies that reflect the requirements of the role.

- Valid and reliable assessments help predict how well, and how safely, someone will perform the tasks of their role.

- Use assessments to measure factors that support on-the-job behaviors and capabilities.

- Easy access to the Internet makes it possible to deliver assessments just about anywhere, from traditional testing centers to kitchen tables.

- Assessment centers offer a wide variety of assessments to evaluate an individual's readiness to perform a new job.

ASSESSING TEAMS

ORGANIZATIONS INCREASINGLY RECOGNIZE that effective teamwork increases engagement, creativity, and productivity. Collaboration is also a plus for team members since they learn so much from working with people who have different skills, experience levels, and perspectives. The devotion of an entire issue of the journal *American Psychologist* in 2018 to the science of teamwork reflected the growing awareness of teamwork's importance in the workplace.

As the pace of technological change increases and systems become more complex, specialists with diverse skillsets and perspectives increasingly will need to work together on various types of teams—sometimes on limited projects, sometimes for many years, across international borders or with people down the hall. Efficient, effective collaboration requires a shared sense of purpose and the willingness to compromise for the good of the team and the achievement of its aims.

The Talent Transformation Pyramid (p. 47) recognizes the crucial role teams play in an organization's overall performance and the need to support the behaviors and attitudes that make teams function well.

As management consultant and author John J. Murphy writes in *Pulling Together: 10 Rules for High-Performance Teamwork*:

To be successful, the team's needs and interests come first. This requires "*we-opic*" vision (What's in it for we?), a challenging step-up from the common "*me-opic*" mindset ... High-performance teams recognize that it takes a joint effort to synergize, generating power above and beyond the collected individuals. It is with the spirit of cooperation that effective teams learn to capitalize on individual strengths and offset individual weaknesses, using diversity as an advantage.

The parameters that impact collective team performance enable members to operate cohesively and coherently—to truly work together. Developing mutual awareness helps team members

- make sense of another's behaviors, adapt to them, and anticipate challenges;

- understand and adjust to another's strengths and shortcomings;

- recognize and adapt to multiple people's knowledge, behaviors, and skills;

- recognize and establish new routines and work rhythms;

- connect emotionally with multiple people simultaneously; and

- respond constructively to feedback.

This chapter examines the making of effective teams and the qualities of great team leaders. We also explore team lifecycles and the typical roles played by team members. We conclude by identifying the kinds of assessments that can help establish strong teams and sustain them as they pursue their objectives.

Understanding Team Leaders

The leaders who build, manage, reform, and disband teams are crucial to their teams' success. With teams taking on greater responsibility for achieving organizations' goals, it's essential to select team leaders carefully and ensure they have the qualities to succeed.

Characteristics of Effective Team Leaders

The recipe for successful leadership depends on the team's mission and objectives. Leaders proven in one sphere might not be successful in another. The qualities someone needs to build a well-funded high-tech unicorn will differ from those for heading a bank or university. Despite these variations, most effective team leaders demonstrate the following qualities, which support behaviors that promote a team's success:

- **Honesty and Trustworthiness:** Team members who know their leader is leveling with them don't waste time and energy trying to figure out what's true.

- **Confidence:** Effective leaders have confidence in their organization's mission and vision and in their ability to help the organization achieve its goals.

- **Supportiveness:** Successful leaders empower team members' collective ability to make decisions together and move things forward—which has the benefit of producing strong support for those decisions among members.

- **Communication:** Effective and timely communication maintains alignment and resolves ambiguities. When faced with new evidence or a changed mission, the leader must engage the team, evaluate the impact, resolve issues, provide clarity, and explain the consequences to the team and internal and external stakeholders.

- **Effective Delegation and Collaboration:** Empowering others to get things done strengthens the team by building members' skills while freeing the leader to oversee what's happening. A leader who creates an environment of transparency, mutual respect, understanding, and trust allows information to flow freely. This empowers members to make decisions with or without the leader's involvement.

Assessing Leadership Skills

Leaders come in all shapes, sizes, and backgrounds, and so do the assessments you can use to evaluate them. Leaders might need to form a new team or take over an existing team; each situation will demand different skillsets and various types of assessments.

Leadership assessments identify an individual's unique characteristics for leading, managing, and directing a project, team, or organization. Before assessing an individual, make sure you understand the personality and behaviors required to take on a project, team, or organization. Document these attributes within a leadership competency model and base your assessments on it.

Leadership assessments generally fall into the following categories:

1. Personality tests that evaluate a leader's traits, values, preferences, motives, style, strengths, and weaknesses

2. 180-degree/360-degree assessments, which discover the opinions of the prospective leader's bosses, colleagues, and direct reports

3. Simulations, which present dilemmas to a prospective leader and evaluate their subsequent behaviors and decisions

See assessments descriptions in Appendix B and a more comprehensive list on the website at www.talentransformation.com/book.

Understanding Teams

Before discussing the kinds of assessments that serve teams best, let's explore what makes teams work effectively.

Characteristics of Effective Teams

Innovative teams reflect a diversity of thought, experience, thinking styles, skills, culture, and age ranges. Diverse teams are most potent when members acknowledge and respect one another's unique experiences, strengths, limitations, and contributions.

Understanding each other's strengths and limitations helps team members naturally determine who should take on which roles and tasks. However, even a diverse, well-rounded team could have individuals who feel they don't fit in or who have trouble cooperating with others. In such cases, the team can prevent or reduce conflict by establishing trust, building mutual respect, and communicating effectively with each other. Assessments—used in conjunction with coaching—can help develop these attributes of a fully functioning, high-performing team.

In addition to diversity, characteristics for effective teams include the following:

- Common purpose
- Shared objectives
- Mutual respect
- Positive relationships
- Complementary skills
- Effective leadership
- Skillful coordination
- Effective decision-making
- Ability to work out disagreements
- Clear communication
- Accountability to one another

The listed characteristics pertain to teamwork, as opposed to group work. Groups are a loose organization of people who coordinate their efforts, whereas a team shares a common purpose, shared objectives, and a strong commitment to reaching them.

Lifecycle

Although some teams have long lives—and a few seem to be permanent fixtures—they follow certain patterns from beginning to dissolution. Assessments can play a valuable role throughout the life of a team, so it's essential to understand this progression. Whether a team forms organically or brings together individuals hand-picked for their respective roles, it requires careful building and nurturing. Members must maintain their shared commitment and hold each other accountable tactfully and sensitively.

Psychologist Bruce Tuckman created a five-stage framework to help us understand the forming and disbanding of a team, with a focus on team dynamics.

1. **Forming:** When individuals come together and are excited but nervous about the work. "Forming" activities include defining the team's purpose, objectives, rules, and processes.

2. **Storming:** When a team has formed, early excitement wanes, and issues emerge. Conflict is most likely at this stage, and team members must learn how to negotiate with each other to get things done.

3. **Norming:** When the team settles into the work, reduces conflict, increases productivity, and comes to terms with its challenges.

4. **Performing:** When the team is working together, getting things done, and team synergy and member satisfaction is high.

5. **Adjourning:** When the project is winding down, and the team must keep working to ensure the quality of the deliverables. This

phase also allows time for the team to reflect on and learn from their experiences.

Figure 7.1 illustrates how to use assessments throughout a team's lifecycle.

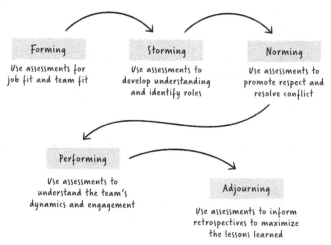

Figure 7.1: Phases of a Team's Lifecycle

Team Roles

It's fair to say that a team leader must understand individual team members before they can understand the team. Considering each one's personality, preferences, experience, communications style, skills, and thought processes can help create a diverse, well-balanced team.

What distinctive roles should team members play? Management theorist Meredith Belbin identifies the following roles for functional teamwork:

- **Completer/Finisher:** A deadline-driven, conscientious champion of quality

- **Coordinator:** An organizer who engages with team members, delegates tasks, and helps the team stay on track

- **Implementer:** A practical strategist who plans for efficient use of resources to achieve the team's objectives

- **Monitor/Evaluator:** A logical, impartial individual who considers options and makes unbiased judgments

- **Plant:** An out-of-the-box thinker who comes up with creative solutions

- **Resource Investigator:** An inquisitive individual who seeks out ideas to share with the team

- **Shaper:** A highly motivated individual who helps the team maintain focus and momentum

- **Specialist:** A domain expert with in-depth knowledge the team requires

- **Teamworker:** A diplomat who helps the team work together to progress toward its objectives

No single management theory is right for every situation, so it's important to choose a model to fit the team's needs. For example, psychologist and consultant Edward de Bono's *Six Thinking Hats* explains distinctive ways for groups to plan detailed thinking processes cohesively. Group behavior theorists Kenneth Benne and Paul Sheats name twenty-six group roles in three categories: task roles, personal/social roles, and dysfunctional/individual roles.

Assigning Responsibilities and Tasks

For a team to be efficient and successful, each member needs to understand their role and responsibilities. A team can assign tasks by dividing the team's responsibilities into separate tasks, analyzing the competencies required for each task, listing the team members' competencies, and matching team members to suitable duties.

The RACI matrix clarifies the responsibility that each individual has for a particular activity or workstream. Specifically, it identifies four types of obligations for an individual or team:

- **Responsible:** One or more people on the team who do the work to complete the task.

- **Accountable:** The person who is ultimately answerable for completing the deliverable or task. This individual delegates, reviews, and signs off on the work. Sometimes, one person on a team fills both the responsible role and the accountable role.

- **Consulted:** Those who provide useful information and advice—typically Subject Matter Experts (SMES)—to support the success of the work. They participate in two-way communication.

- **Informed:** Team members who receive updates on the team's work but do not get involved in the details of every deliverable.

Team Assessments

To build the team and assign appropriate roles and tasks, a team leader may want to get a feel for individual and team behaviors and capabilities, as well as members' ability to get things done and achieve objectives. Assessing members' personalities, values, beliefs, and preferences offers a means of predicting behaviors. To predict capabilities, the leader should understand individuals' technical skills and the environment in which they will be working. Having gained a sense of members' likely behaviors and capabilities, the leader can promote learning experiences to resolve areas of concern.

A team leader is responsible for assembling a team with the competencies required to achieve its objectives.

Assessing each member's personality, style, and strengths can help a team leader identify roles that would suit them and can help team members better understand themselves and each other.

Evaluating each member's technical skills, professional experience, and ability to use tools helps the leader identify appropriate roles and tasks for them.

Figure 7.2 shows how an individual's competencies (their behaviors and capabilities) compare to the team's.

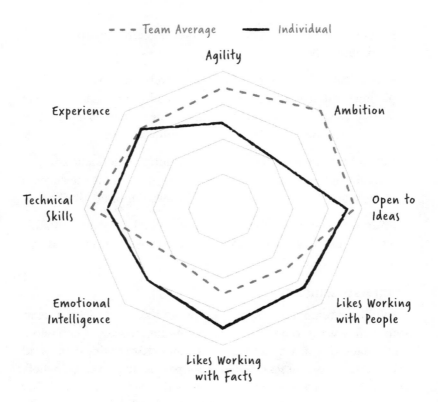

Figure 7.2: An Individual's Behaviors
and Capabilities within a Team

A team's ability to achieve objectives will depend on how well the members work together. Success requires clarity of purpose, vision, trust, understanding, effective communications, commitment, willingness to be held accountable, and a desire to succeed.

Figure 7.3 shows how one team member's attributes might contribute to the entire team's success.

We noted earlier that assessment is vital throughout a team's lifecycle. Let's explore assessments for identifying team members' styles, evaluating how they work together, and addressing problems.

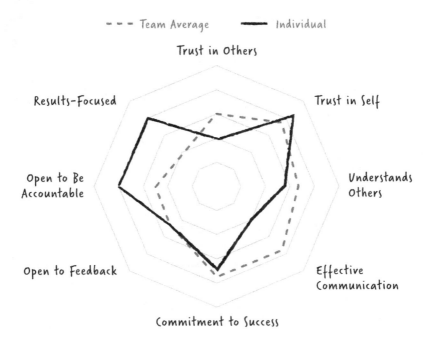

Figure 7.3: An Individual's Attributes
Compared to the Team's

Identifying Team Members' Personal Styles

Assessments that explore prospective team members' personal styles—including their social, behavioral, communication, and conflict management styles—can help ensure the creation of a well-balanced team. Such assessments also promote team members' understanding of each other. This understanding helps them develop mutual respect, which in turn creates harmony, reduces stress, improves productivity, and boosts morale. Team members who understand each other well are more apt to work together effectively, make sound decisions, and develop creative solutions to the challenges they face.

Figure 7.4 shows ways to represent personal style assessment results on a 2D grid:

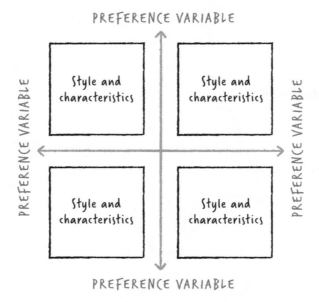

Figure 7.4.1: Dimensions of Personal Styles

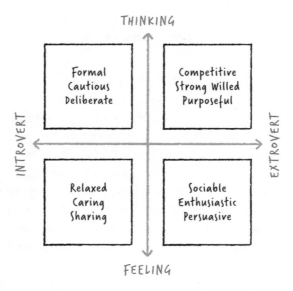

Figure 7.4.2: An Example of Personal Styles

The X and Y axes stand for two measurable personal styles. Here are some examples:

- **Personal Style:** Introversion/extraversion versus thinking/feeling

- **Social Style:** Assertiveness versus emotional control

- **Behavioral Style:** Responsiveness versus assertiveness

- **Communication Style:** Openness versus directness

- **Leadership Style:** Support versus direction

- **Conflict Management Style:** Assertive/compromising versus competing/cooperative

- **Personality Style:** Introversion/extraversion versus sensing/intuition

Figure 7.5 illustrates how the results of a style assessment would appear as plotted on a graph representing the team's dynamics:

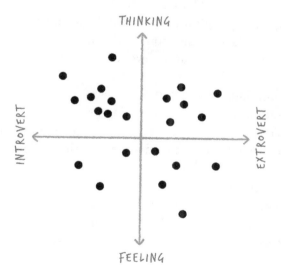

Figure 7.5: Example of Distribution
of Personal Styles within a Team

Evaluating How Well a Team Works Together

A team's success represents the sum of its parts, so it's essential to assess the members' characteristics and behaviors in terms of how they contribute to the team. Here are examples of meaningful things to measure when evaluating how a team functions:

1. Trust between team members, based on integrity, competence, reliability, and empathy

2. Fear of conflict, which might prevent team members from sharing new ideas or exposing useful challenges

3. Level of commitment to an assignment

4. Willingness to be held accountable

5. Focus on getting results

Surveys can provide valuable information about how teams are functioning. These include pulse surveys that ask one quick question, short-form surveys with up to ten items, or long-form surveys. Gauging opinions, monitoring levels of engagement, and evaluating people's levels of satisfaction provide insights that can prompt appropriate interventions and course corrections.

Determining Sources of Problems

Assessments can help identify and diagnose underlying problems in teams. The results of those assessments can help determine what interventions would help team members set things right.

Among Team Members

Suppose team members who share the same workspace struggle with interpersonal issues or disagreements. Conversations about mutual respect and an assessment of conflict resolution styles might help here, as could revisiting the results of previous personality assessments to renew team members' awareness of each other's preferences. The team leader plays a vital role in evaluating what's going on and determining how to help team members demonstrate mutual respect. If conflicts remain unresolved, it could be that the leader needs to improve through further assessment and intervention.

If a geographically distant team member feels excluded and consequently drops back from full participation, the team leader needs to act. Informed by findings from the original assessments of each team member's personality, the leader should address the person and say, in effect, "We have not been hearing from you, and we value your contributions."

With the Leader

Assessing how a team leader makes decisions, implements plans, and motivates others can identify the person's strengths, weaknesses, and opportunities for improvement. Combining coaching with 180-degree and 360-degree assessments based on a well-understood competency model can help a leader learn and develop leadership skills while on the job.

When to Assess Teams

Experts recommend using assessment early in a team's life, but later stages merit their use too.

Teams in Formation

A team leader can help members get off on the right foot by learning about each other's strengths and establish a shared vocabulary during the formative stage. Straightforward personality, strength-finder, and emotional intelligence assessments help people understand themselves and others. Assessing team members' styles regarding behavior, communication, and leadership can also help team members get to know each other and anticipate how they will probably interact. This mutual understanding could help prevent conflicts from developing.

Assessments also can refresh or strengthen the team as their work progresses. As new people join, repeating some team assessments might help the newcomers gain the same insights as the original members.

Cross-functional Teams

When teams come together to work on a project, they create a team made up of teams! In these situations, consider using easy-to-understand assessments to promote similar understandings just as you would within a single team: personality, style, emotional intelligence, and strength-finder assessments that help people understand themselves and others.

Established Teams

Once teams are up and running, there may not be a great need to run assessments. But when a team's effectiveness and productivity lag—or when a team is working under unusual circumstances—assessments can help establish a sense of direction and build cohesiveness. Depending on the situation and the team members involved, it usually falls to the leader to evaluate the evidence judiciously and use whatever assessments and interventions they believe will help keep the team on track.

Here are some circumstances that call for assessments and consequent interventions:

Trust Issues

Trust is foundational for team performance. Without it, teams can't work at their full potential. Assessments of trust help team leaders and members evaluate such things as members' willingness to admit mistakes, ask for help, and acknowledge their weaknesses. Team-building activities and games allow members to learn more about each other and establish closer bonds through collaboration and fun competition.

Lack of a Shared Vision

A team cannot work effectively without a shared vision and a mutual understanding of its purpose. All members should be on board with the deliverables that management expects from them, the milestones they need to achieve, and the reason they are going to all this effort. At times, team members may sense the absence of a shared vision or purpose but can't figure out the root cause of that disconnect. Lack of mutual trust could be a factor, for example, as could lack of leadership, poor communication, different perspectives on the organization's mission, disagreements about the team's role in achieving it, or a need to change course and establish a new sense of direction. Frank conversations can help team members harvest insights into the underlying issues, as can assessments of understanding, respect, and trust. If a change of course is in order due to changes in circumstances or organizational priorities, the leader can engage the team in setting new priorities and aligning their roles, plans, and tasks to the new vision.

Healthy versus Unhealthy Conflict

Highly effective teams welcome healthy conflict, which demonstrates buy-in and commitment by team members and reflects their desire to improve outcomes. Healthy conflict requires openness, tact, and willingness to listen to other people's ideas. Putting ego aside and aiming for the higher good yields positive results. But when conflict devolves into personal attacks, defensiveness, and competition, it becomes an unhealthy source of distraction and negativity.

According to business management author Patrick Lencioni, fear of conflict holds teams back by pasting over contentious issues with a false impression of harmony. In his book, *The Five Dysfunctions of a Team: A Leadership Fable,* Lencioni identifies these roadblocks to success:

- **Absence of Trust:** Unwillingness to be *vulnerable* within the group.

- **Fear of Conflict:** Preferring *artificial harmony* to constructive debate.

- **Lack of Commitment:** Feigning buy-in for group decisions, which creates *ambiguity*.

- **Avoidance of Accountability:** Avoiding the need to call peers out on counterproductive behavior.

- **Inattention to Results:** Focusing on personal success, status, and ego before team success.

Teams can counter these dysfunctions by cultivating a strong sense of trust and communicating openly. These two accomplishments build the commitment and accountability that yield positive results, as illustrated in Figure 7.6:

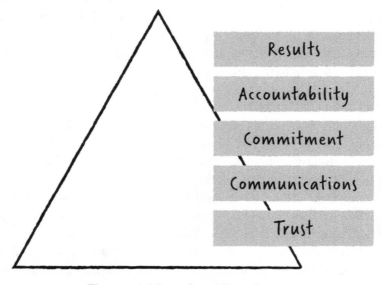

Figure 7.6: Hierarchy of Team Success

Dispersed Teams

Building productive teams of remote workers starts with selecting individuals who have strong communication and collaboration skills and would naturally thrive as remote workers. Personality tests can help the leader identify people who are likely to respond constructively to a lack of personal contact.

Successful remote workers stay focused, use their time efficiently, and work autonomously. They also reach out when they need help, write and speak tactfully, and proactively engage with their colleagues. Team leaders can add to the sense of connection by reaching out to team members individually and bringing the team together regularly to check in with each other. COVID-19 heightened the need to understand and support people working apart from one another.

The human connections that happen naturally within a physical location must be more deliberate among dispersed teams. Assessments can build team members' awareness of their personality types, emotional intelligence, and strengths. Still, the inability to observe colleagues' body language or strike up spontaneous conversations calls for extra effort.

Here are some ways to encourage engagement and strengthen connections:

- Encourage everyone to speak to the group at the beginning of each call.

- Break the ice by having a team member share a link to an article or video and explain why they found the content helpful.

- Use video, sustained chat, shared directories, and other communication tools to ease collaboration.

- Communicate clearly about performance metrics.

- Hold regular conference calls to review the team's performance and explain how this supports the organization's objectives.

- Build relationships in a fun way by playing interactive team-building games.

Takeaways

- Assessments for team leaders should align with a competency model based on the requirements of the job.

- Innovative teams reflect a diversity of thought, experience, thinking styles, skills, culture, and age ranges.

- Personality, strength-finder, and emotional intelligence assessments can inform team selection and help team members understand themselves and others.

- While assessments play a crucial role during team formation, they can also help established teams regain their sense of direction when faced with lagging productivity, conflicts, and other stresses.

- Members of dispersed teams need more support than those on site to forge robust connections and stay engaged.

8

IMPROVING
ORGANIZATIONAL
RESULTS

W
E HAVE SEEN in previous chapters that new working practices and technologies are changing the way organizations
assess talent. Similar changes are happening in the way
they track metrics and detect correlations that inform and
improve their decision-making. Organizations can now use the
Talent Transformation Pyramid (p. 47) to identify correlations
between mindset, skillset, and performance. Then they can detect
causation and choose interventions that will boost results.

The evolution of organizations from vertical, top-down management to horizontal management models has put more responsibility
into the hands of workers. The autocratic management methodol-
ogy of the past tended to inhibit engagement and innovation. But
today's creative, collaborative environment empowers employees to
determine how they will help an organization achieve its goals. New
approaches that make for a more stimulating work-life also call for
an organization to monitor its progress toward achieving its vision,
mission, and cultural objectives.

In this chapter, we discuss the importance of identifying sound goals and tracking progress using Key Performance Indicators (KPIS) and other methods. We also discuss some approaches to establishing business models, setting objectives, measuring performance outcomes, and checking on progress.

Goals versus Objectives

We can't help talking about goals and objectives in a chapter about improvement, but these terms sometimes cause confusion. Although many people use them interchangeably and they seem similar, we differentiate them in this book. When we mention "goals," we are referring to SMART goals, which must possess the following characteristics:

- Specific
- Measurable
- Actionable
- Realistic
- Timebound

While objectives are timebound, they are unlike SMART goals in that they are not necessarily specific, measurable, actionable, and realistic. For example, an objective might be to "improve customer satisfaction this quarter," whereas a SMART goal might be to "increase Net Promoter Scores (NPS) to >80 in this quarter by providing new knowledge bases to help customer service representatives and resolve issues on the first call."

In addition to these distinctions, we write about goals and objectives in different contexts. We relate goals to KPIS and write about Objectives and Key Results (OKRs), a management tool for focusing on specific issues to change an organization, product, or service.

Later in the chapter, we provide more details about OKRs. For now, let's explore the relationship between KPIS and goals.

Key Performance Indicators (KPIs)

KPIs are measurements for monitoring an organization's progress toward its goals. They are useful not only for measuring current performance and tracking progress against a plan, but also for monitoring the changes that occur as an organization pursues any type of transformation. Tracking KPIs will help your organization determine whether change is happening as planned. As the saying attributed to W. Edwards Deming and Peter Drucker goes, "You can't manage what you can't measure."

Organizations use standard KPIs—such as revenue, overheads, and profit—and develops situation-specific, in-house KPIs to manage their operations effectively. Typically, each department or team monitors their own KPIs to ensure they are on track to achieve their goals. To brainstorm potential KPIs, ask the question, "What number will change if we are successful?" As you define each KPI, identify the data source and reporting frequency along with the target to reduce the potential ambiguity of tracking a KPI over a long period. As an example, if you are trying to increase revenues by running a promotion, you would track in the accounting system the revenue generated from that promotion daily or weekly.

There are too many KPIs to list within this chapter, so we've provided a table on our website at www.talenttransformation.com/book. There, we include numerous examples to stimulate ideas about the various KPIs you could use.

Selecting the Right KPIs

Albert Einstein noted, "Not everything that can be counted counts, and not everything that counts can be counted." Instead of counting everything you can, focus on your organization's transformational, strategic initiatives and choose KPIs that relate directly to them. These KPIs should align all individuals and teams to move consistently in the desired direction.

KPIs should be specific enough so that those who influence a metric can correlate their activities to it. As an example, compensating customer service for sales revenues they can't directly influence would be demotivating. Instead, track a customer service team's impact on metrics for NPS or fix-on-first call.

To ensure clarity for those who will impact the metric, it is best to select just three to eight KPIs for each individual or team. Ideally, one of these will be a "north star" metric, which can indicate whether the plan or overall transformation is on target.

Here are ten guidelines to help you select the KPIs that will be the most meaningful for your organization:

1. Choose KPIs that align with strategic transformation objectives.

2. Make sure your KPIs have a defined and causal relationship to the objective.

3. Select indicators that will predict a future outcome.

4. Use KPIs people can trust and understand.

5. Select KPIs that represent the required transformations.

6. Use data from sources you trust.

7. Consider the cost of data acquisition in selecting KPIs.

8. Make KPIs specific enough to inform particular actions.

9. Confirm what activities could influence the KPI.

10. Kill off KPIs that aren't helping.

Please note: Metrics to track talent transformation are different from those for monitoring operations. Also, you should independently track transformational initiatives that might not impact organizational KPIS quickly. For example, if you measure leadership development as being delivered and new skills as being used, those KPIS might not affect your organization's balanced scorecard for months or years.

Enable Stakeholders to Monitor KPIS

Informing employees, team leaders, managers, and other stakeholders helps everyone track progress and focus on the KPIs they can influence. Here are some steps you can take to loop everyone in:

1. Determine which KPIs you want to track.

2. Discover and deploy the technology and processes needed to access the data regularly.

3. Create dashboards where people can select the KPIs they want to see regularly.

4. Allow users to drill down on the KPIs they are monitoring.

Using Dashboards

As we mentioned in Chapter 3, customizable dashboards can help you see at a glance what's happening across your organization or in individual departments. You can display a variety of metrics to help you follow KPIs to pinpoint trouble spots and take action. Checking dashboards at least weekly, you can note the progress you've made toward key results and your quarterly goals. Figure 8.1 shows a typical dashboard element that displays a KPI against its target.

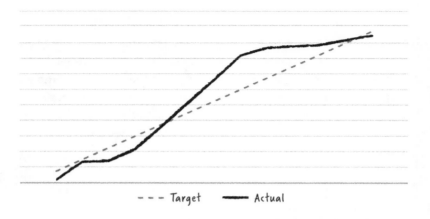

Figure 8.1: Tracking a KPI against Target

Dashboards can:

- show you how far along you should be at any point in the quarter or year;

- compare your current progress to your expectations;

- note when you have reached or exceeded your goals; and/or

- nudge you if you're falling behind.

Making Sense of Organizational Metrics

Before you set out to measure your organization's performance, consider using a framework to group metrics into an understandable form. With an organized model representing the data, leaders can pinpoint the sources of issues and take the most appropriate action. One such framework is Alexander Osterwalder's business model canvas, developed in 2005 (Figure 8.2) and now used by many types of organizations.

Like the Talent Transformation Pyramid, the business model canvas will help you visualize something you cannot see. The canvas promotes an understanding of the interplay among an organization's various functions. While the pyramid displays factors related to talent, the business model canvas depicts the functions that will impact organizational performance.

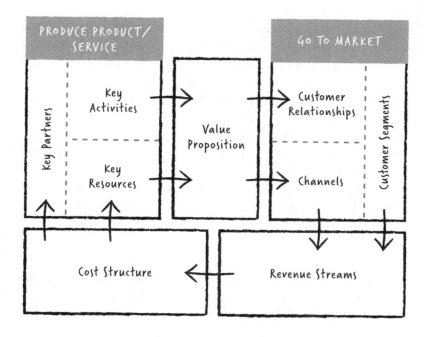

Figure 8.2: Osterwalder's Business Model Canvas

You can tailor these components of the business model canvas to the needs of your organization.

Goods and services are packaged into a value proposition and then go to market. The revenue generated from clients feeds into the organization's cost structure, which in turn feeds the production process. Here are descriptions of each aspect of the canvas:

Key Partners

Organizations partner with individuals, businesses, not-for-profit organizations, academic institutions, and governments to further their mutual interests. For example, an organization might collaborate with a nonprofit to develop industry standards or satisfy their social responsibilities. They might partner with schools, colleges, and universities to help build a pipeline of talent for years to come. They might partner to obtain goods or services to support or complement their offering to their clients. Other forms of partnerships—such as joint ventures and strategic alliances—enable the partners to leverage the synergies of their relationship to further their objectives. Equity partners might provide capital to help an organization fund its growth. In coming together, partners might establish success metrics upfront and enhance them as the partnership develops.

Examples of KPIs that measure this function are partner satisfaction, investor's internal rate of return, speed to hire, and size of talent pipeline.

Key Activities

Organizations perform activities to provide value to their clients. Activities might be manufacturing components or products, developing systems and processes, or providing support services.

Timeliness and quality are the measures of activities: Are the products or services delivered on time? And did they meet the required standard?

Examples of KPIs that measure this function are errors evident in procured goods, errors evident in production, and fix-on-first call.

Key Resources

To perform their activities and provide value to their clients, organizations need resources. These include intellectual property, financial resources, physical assets, human resources, and systems and processes. Intellectual property, which an organization might own or have licensed, enables it to provide unique products and services.

Financial resources allow an organization to invest in developing its people, products, and services to increase the value proposition that it offers to its clients. Physical assets, such as buildings, machines, and vehicles, enable an organization to develop, manufacture, and offer its products and services to its clients. Human resources are the people who perform tasks. Systems and processes enable the organization to perform its activities efficiently.

Examples of KPIs that measure this function are patents owned, employee satisfaction, employee count, processes handled by automation, and processes handled by people.

Value Proposition

An organization's value proposition is the value that it provides for its clients.

Here are two examples:

1. A toothbrush makes it easy to clean your teeth. It's not too soft, not too hard, and priced to be disposable and inexpensive to replace with a new one. The availability of various shapes, sizes, packaging, and prices offer value propositions for specific consumer preferences.

2. Executive coaching can enhance a leader's performance so much that the cost can be insignificant compared to their improved ability to better their organization's performance. Executive coaches can link their value proposition to an hourly fee or a KPI that the leader wants to change.

The client's perspective and priorities determine the measurement of the value proposition. Clients might look to increase their own revenues, reduce their costs, improve their efficiency, or take advantage of new opportunities. As an example, an organization providing background checks on job candidates might help their clients improve their recruitment success by providing a bundle of services that includes criminal background checks, academic credential confirmation, and drug screening. These services might deliver immense value to their clients. For consumers, the value proposition is more personal. The person who buys that toothbrush we just mentioned might be looking for whiter teeth, healthier gums, or a decreased risk of painful dental procedures.

Examples of KPIs that measure this function are time to purchase, purchase frequency, repeat purchases, lifetime value, gross profit, and customer acquisition cost.

Customer Relationships

Positive relationships with prospective customers are essential to an organization's success. These relationships might rely on social media and branding or more personal and intimate engagements. A variety of sources yield data for measuring customer satisfaction, sentiment, and engagement. These sources might include interactions with social media, websites, contact centers, phone, email, chat systems, orders, returns, focus groups, and surveys.

To assess the quality of your organization's customer relationships, you need data that measures customer engagement and predicts customer retention, purchasing habits, and future needs.

Examples of KPIs that measure this function are customer satisfaction, customers retained, customers lost, and engagement.

Customer Segments

Organizations often have multiple customer segments that find one value proposition more appealing than another, or that prefer different styles of relationships. Customer segmentation takes many forms and helps an organization determine how to present its value proposition to and engage with a particular type of customer. For instance, a manufacturer of cleaning supplies would present its product differently to consumers, hospitals, and hotel chains. Although the underlying product is the same, the value proposition is different for each market sector. You might segment your market by geography, demographics, industry type, or some other category. Customer segmentation not only enables an organization to package its products and services by market; it also allows organizations to measure satisfaction and return on investment by market. In this way, customer segmentation helps organizations select the markets that they want to be in and fine-tune their value proposition for each.

Examples of KPIs that measure this function are total addressable market, customer satisfaction, and return on investment.

Channels

Channels are the methods organizations can use to bring their products to market. There are three broad types of channels (see Figure 8.3): Businesses sell directly to consumers using a B2C channel, to another business using a B2B channel, and to government entities using a B2G channel. Makers of consumer products tend to distribute their wares via retails stores and e-commerce outlets such as Amazon. Some organizations, such as government agencies or certain nonprofits, might have specific purchasing requirements, such as buying from minority-owned businesses, and might purchase goods via an intermediary to meet the contracting requirements.

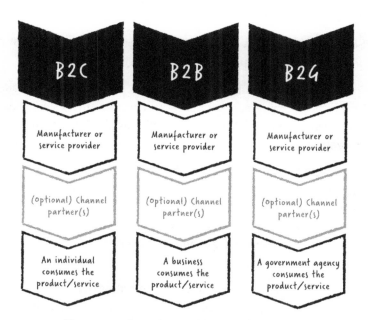

Figure 8.3: Overview of Channels to Market

Measuring channel metrics is mostly a matter of measuring the quantity of goods or services sold, revenue, profitability, and customer satisfaction. If and when the channel adds value to the purchase by offering, say, installation and maintenance services, the manufacturer might also track the quality of service provided.

Examples of KPIs that measure this function are investment made by the business itself, investment made by a channel partner, leads from either side, sales revenues, certifications, and client satisfaction.

Revenue Streams

Organizations earn revenues by providing products or services that may be categorized by geography, channel, and the types of revenue:

- Transactional revenues come from simple purchases of a product or service. The customer has no ongoing obligation to consume more or pay more. Revenues from the purchase of clothes or groceries are examples of transactional revenues.

- Services revenues involve a client buying a one-time service such as a day at a health spa or the translation of a document.

- Project-based revenues are often billed and paid for in phases. Often they are payments for creative services such as creating a marketing campaign, developing software, building a structure, or providing industrial design.

- Subscription or recurring revenues are earned by providing an ongoing product or service in exchange for ongoing fees. Examples of subscriptions include charges for business software packages, print magazines, and gym memberships. Tutoring, cleaning, and building maintenance are examples of services generating recurring revenues.

- Additional revenues from non-core activities that do not fit into revenue streams might include receipts from interest, dividends, and rents.

Revenue streams are measured against projections, targets, and market potential.

Examples of KPIs that measure this function are revenue by product, revenue by service, revenue by market, revenue by geography, and annual recurring revenue.

Cost Structure

Paying bills for fixed and variable costs is a necessary part of running an organization. Fixed costs include those for product and service development, salaries, rent, insurance, advertising, utilities, training, office expenses, and the infrastructure required to support the organization. These costs are often referred to as overheads and remain fixed regardless of revenues. Variable costs are those that vary for each product sold. As an example, each refrigerator sold has a cost associated with the components required to assemble and ship it, the "cost of goods."

KPIs that measure this function are cost of goods, gross profit, fixed costs, variable costs, revenue targets, and performance against budget.

Measuring Organizational Performance

Setting goals and managing client, employee, and other stakeholder expectations is essential to running a successful organization. Setting goals for budgets, revenue, profit/loss, delivery dates, customer satisfaction, and employee engagement are ways to explain the organization's vision and provide numbers to benchmark performance.

The business model canvas just discussed is one method of categorizing metrics within a framework, assessing your organization's performance, and making improvements. But there are many other ways to monitor progress. For example, an investor will be attentive to financial metrics, a manufacturer will be interested in quality metrics, and philanthropic institutions will be concerned about their impact on the public good.

As each organization is unique, you may well use different systems to track specific metrics and the progress of individuals, teams, and your entire organization. However, these basic principles of measuring performance outcomes apply to everyone:

1. Understand your organization's vision, mission, and purpose.

2. Establish SMART goals that will help you fulfill all three.

3. Set and manage realistic expectations.

4. Determine what you need to measure as you reach toward each goal.

5. Measure your progress consistently and make changes accordingly.

6. Identify multiple performance indicators that make sense for your organization.

7. Monitor these indicators and correlate them with other metrics.

8. Keep checking to ensure that you are measuring what matters.

There are myriad ways to set up your organization's system for setting goals and tracking progress toward them. Here are some tried and tested examples.

Objectives and Key Results (OKR)
OKR is a framework that helps you document what you want to achieve and measure your progress. Using this framework, you can define what you need to accomplish in each period and set up ways to track your steps toward those achievements.

Former Intel President and CEO Andrew Grove invented OKRs and wrote about them in his 1983 book, *High Output Management*. Kleiner Perkins Chairman John Doerr then introduced the OKR framework to Google, whose cofounder Larry Page credited it with keeping the company on track and contributing to its dramatic growth. Observing Google's success, many tech and non-tech companies have adopted OKR as a management tool. Doerr's 2018 book,

Measure What Matters: How Google, Bono, and the Gates Foundation Rock the World with OKRs, explains how to implement the OKR system and provides examples of organizations that have used them to improve performance.

Sharing OKRs across your organization will help teams align with each other and focus their efforts on initiatives that will help the enterprise reach its goals.

OKRs combine an objective with clearly defined key results—sets of metrics for measuring the achievement of each objective. You must support your objectives with initiatives, plans, and activities that will help you achieve the required key results (see Figure 8.4).

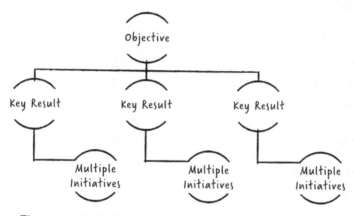

Figure 8.4: Initiatives and Key Results Support Objectives

Set Objectives

Objectives are significant aims for your organization to achieve in a time period. Having well-defined objectives keeps your thinking clear and gives you a steady sense of direction.

Here are some examples of objectives:

- Delight clients this quarter with the amazing new product released last month.

- Maximize and sustain recurring revenues this year.

- This quarter create standard contracts that are easy to agree to.

- Achieve sustainable and environmentally friendly growth within five years.

- Become the employer of choice by the end of the year.

Define Key Results

A key result is a tool for improving the performance of a particular metric. Unlike KPIs, which represent what is happening at any given time and generally help you track progress, key results pertain to a specific timeframe.

Key results usually include these elements:

- **Title:** The key result's name, which could be as simple as KR1.

- **Metric:** The measure that the key result documents.

- **Start Value:** The value of the metric at the start of the period, which helps everyone understand how challenging the key result is. The value you start with also avoids ambiguities, especially when using percentages of previous values.

- **Target Value:** The value you want that metric to have at the end of your timeframe.

Examples of commonly used metrics include NPS, Employee Net Promoter Score (eNPS), Monthly Active Users (MAU), Monthly Recurring Revenue (MRR), churn rate, new customer leads, blog subscribers, and attendance at trade shows.

You can measure key results on a 0–100 percent scale or use any numeric unit (such as dollar amount, items, scores, and so on).

For example, if your objective is to delight clients with an amazing new product that was released last month, your key results might look like this:

- **KR:** "Net Promoter Score": NPS for new product is >70 during the quarter (NPS was 65 last quarter).

- **KR:** "Online Review": >25 new and positive online reviews from clients in the first month of the quarter.

- **KR:** "First-month usage": Monthly Active Users are >5,000 during first month of quarter.

- **KR:** "Third-month usage": Monthly Active Users >20,000 during third month of quarter.

If your objective is to create standard contracts that are easy to agree to, your key results might look like this:

- **KR:** "Contracts Available": All contracts to be updated by legal and published before the end of first month of the quarter (25 contracts need updating).

- **KR:** "Sales Trained": Sales team are trained on new contracts by the end of first month of the quarter (70 people need training).

- **KR:** "Questions to Legal": Questions escalated to legal are <75/week in the second month of the quarter (current escalations average 174/week).

- **KR:** "Questions to Legal": Total number of questions escalated to legal in the quarter are <200 (current escalations average 748/quarter).

Balanced Scorecard

With so many measures available, focusing on one set over another can be risky. For example, you could prioritize customer service over financial metrics and go out of business. Or you could focus on financial metrics and fail to invest adequate resources in upskilling, resulting in declining customer service. You can avoid these pitfalls by using the balanced scorecard, which Robert S. Kaplan and David P. Norton developed in the nineties. This management tool helps organizations categorize their goals into one of four domains to determine if the domains are appropriately balanced:

1. **Financial** goals identify measures that would represent commercial success, such as cash flow, sales growth, operating income, return on equity, and gross profit.

2. **Customer** goals identify metrics that signal client satisfaction, such as NPS, percent of sales from new products, market share, and on-time delivery.

3. **Internal business processes** goals represent measures related to operational excellence such as cycle time, speed to market, unit cost, yield, new product introductions, and service levels.

4. **Learning and growth** goals identify measures of human resources such as employee competencies, employee engagement, employee turnover, eNPS, and the number of employees certified.

A scorecard presents KPIs in a way that makes it easy to monitor progress against goals. Scores in red could show that the indicators are off target, and scores in green could show that they are on target. Figure 8.5 depicts a black and white example of a balanced scorecard.

Domain	Goals	Q1				Q2			
		Target	Actual	Status	Trend	Target	Actual	Status	Trend
Financial	Increase ARR (in $'000)	$1,000	$1,050	✓	↑	$1,100	$1,075	✗	→
Financial	Customer Acquisition Cost (CAC)	$750	$975	✗	↓	$750	$895	✗	↓
Financial	Increase revenue/sale	$269	$245	✗	↑	$272	$273	✓	↑
Customer	Customer Satisfaction (NPS)	75	68	✗	↑	77	74	✗	↑
Customer	Customer Retention (CRR)	95.6%	96.0%	✓	↓	95.6%	94.0%	✗	↑
Customer	Chatbot Success Rate	75.0%	65.1%	✗	↑	75.0%	69.8%	✗	↑
Systems and Processes	Processes handled by automation	1,000	908	✗	↑	1,200	1,106	✗	↑
Systems and Processes	Automate expense processing	25%	35%	✓	↑	50%	55%	✓	↑
Systems and Processes	# of calls to contact center (new App)	800	759	✓	↓	700	674	✓	↓
Learning and Growth	Employee Net Promoter Score (eNPS)	75	62	✗	↑	75	68	✗	↑
Learning and Growth	Internal + External certifications completed	1,000	500	✗	↑	1,000	769	✗	↑
Learning and Growth	Regretted turnover	25	14	✓	↑	25	28	✗	↓

Figure 8.5: Example of a Balanced Scorecard
(✓ = on target; X = off target)

Takeaways

- This book differentiates goals and objectives by reserving the word "goals" for SMART goals, which must be specific, measurable, actionable, realistic, and timebound.

- KPIS are metrics that help individuals, teams, and organizations focus on the numbers that matter.

- Displaying metrics within a framework such as the business model canvas provides a comprehensive guide for tracking performance.

- Use Objectives and Key Results (OKRS) to document the desired changes and measure your progress.

- Dashboards, such as the balanced scorecard, aid focus by representing essential metrics in an understandable form.

LOOKING AHEAD

W E CANNOT OFFER a detailed blueprint for the future of work, but we can point to trends, technologies, and necessities that will shape it. Some developments may surprise us. COVID-19 certainly did, moving millions of office workers into their homes and making online meetings commonplace.

In this chapter, we explore four trends that will change the new world of work. We also describe the future of learning and discuss how assessment data, correlated with other information and supported by sophisticated analysis, will improve decision-making.

Four Trends Driving Exponential Change

The way we live, learn, and work is changing rapidly. We have identified four clear trends that are driving this change:

1. Blended technologies
2. Innovative business models
3. A growing emphasis on social responsibility
4. New ways to nurture and inspire talent

Blended Technologies

Any new technology triggers uncertainty and requires agility in our response—including new skills for its development, maintenance, and deployment. As technologies combine, they develop synergy, multiplying their capabilities, power, influence, and impact. This, in turn, drives massive changes that force organizations—and their workers—to change along with them.

The traditional, 2D world of data entry and reports has given way to complex combinations of technologies that enable everything from voice-activated grocery shopping to wearable biological sensors. The ability to collect and analyze massive amounts of data is at the heart of these developments. Powerful technological combinations also impact the work world.

Package delivery does not rely on a single innovation. The drone balances itself in flight with the help of gyroscopes, Artificial Intelligence (AI), and geo-mapping. It reports its speed, position, potential hazards, and other conditions in real time to the control center. The drone has some autonomy but tried-and-true communication technologies control it from afar. The drone's robust construction from new, lightweight materials, as well as powerful batteries, help make it viable for delivering packages.

Machine Learning (ML) gathers comprehensive data and uses powerful algorithms to analyze it. Organizations can use this technology to

- evaluate patterns of customer behavior to review and modify sales and marketing strategies;

- identify high-risk medical patients and prevent data-entry duplication and inaccuracy;

- detect fraud;

- improve spam filters; and/or

- enhance predictive maintenance in manufacturing plants.

See the Glossary of Technologies in Appendix A and on our website at www.talenttransformation.com/book for details about technologies that are enabling massive changes in the work world.

Innovative Business Models

Technological and societal changes have introduced new approaches to doing business. Organizations are veering away from traditional, vertically structured management models that put business functions into independent silos. Instead, they are embracing horizontal models offering more agile ways of working, sharing information, and collaborating between functions. As an example, an organization can improve its value proposition by harvesting data from smart devices to enable rapid and data-driven decision-making about consumer behaviors. Sharing data to enhance products, services, supply chain management, quality, efficiency, and performance can improve business-to-business relationships. For instance, a trucking company could send the vehicle manufacturer data about the use of its vehicles, and the manufacturer could suggest ways to improve vehicle maintenance.

Here are some creative, responsive business models that reflect the influence of consumer and client behaviors as well as new technological capabilities.

Consumption-Based Pricing

Instead of buying things, people are increasingly seeking ways to pay only for what they use. The popularity of ridesharing apps exemplifies this. Instead of paying to own a car, or even to lease one, people jump into someone else's car and pay only to get where they need to go. Other examples of consumption-based pricing include clothing rentals and subscriptions, music streaming, video-on-demand, and the provision of software, platforms, hardware, and infrastructure as services instead of purchases.

Personalization and Customer Experience

Influenced by online shopping and video-on-demand, many consumers and clients now expect personalized experiences. In response, many other sectors are providing unique buying experiences, both on the ground and online. As an example, people shopping for cars appreciate marketing, advertising, and interactions that resonate with their wants and needs. Data analytics and effective personal communication make this work. Car dealerships need accurate datasets (powered by AI) to ensure they know enough about their customers to communicate productively with them. Digital sales and marketing are increasingly personal too. When your digital assistant reminds you that you ordered dog food a month ago and asks if you need more, that's personalized shopping.

Decision-makers will need to balance customers' preferences with the capabilities of technology. Some customers will value the efficiency of ordering their restaurant meal on a tablet, but others may wish for the personal attention of a waiter. Some will be delighted to have a robot mix them a cocktail, but can the robot take the place of a simpatico bartender? Technology brings potential new approaches to balancing price, intimacy, and speed, but getting that equation right will call for a clear understanding of one's customers.

Data-driven Decision-making

As we have seen from the COVID-19 pandemic, data is strategically essential. The ability to use data to model potential impacts empowers decision-makers to position regions, countries, organizations, teams, and individuals for success. Leaders who collect and analyze data via online marketplaces and the Internet of Things (IoT) will be able to predict revenues, potential product acceptance, and customer satisfaction with more certainty. Collecting data from people and devices also makes it easier to plan and implement new strategies and detect their impact.

Online Marketplaces

Just as stock markets moved online decades ago, many products and services of the physical world have now moved online. Innovative marketplaces are springing up for secondhand furniture, used books, artwork, ridesharing, garage sales, mortgages, and healthcare. These gathering places empower buyers and sellers to set their prices in response to supply and demand.

Talent marketplaces, whether for freelancers or employees, provide information to help organizations differentiate between candidates. These marketplaces might offer assessments to determine potential job fit. They also might report credentials or microcredentials that document individuals' skills and knowledge.

A Growing Emphasis on Social Responsibility

As science increasingly reveals the impact of industry on the planet, consumers and investors are calling for organizations to reduce their emissions, use resources responsibly, connect with their communities, and contribute to the lives of the less fortunate. An organization boosts its health, reputation, and bottom line by being socially responsible. Social networks, comparison websites, and online shopping enable us to evaluate suppliers in new ways. Organizations must be clear about their social responsibilities to maintain and enhance their reputation in the eyes of their customers. The following aspects of good corporate citizenship will grow more significant as the demand for social responsibility increases.

Health and Safety

Organizations have long maintained policies and procedures to prevent employee injury and promote employee health. But the scope of health and safety policies has grown to include infection control, mental health, and many other concerns. COVID-19 has accelerated this trend by necessitating stricter public health practices. Health education, hand hygiene, cleaning and disinfecting, vaccinations, data monitoring, and careful maintenance of heating and cooling systems are high on the list.

Organizations' heightened responsibility for ensuring safe working environments will apply whether people work alone or in partnership with machines. Keeping employees safe requires continued diligence as people work alongside or inside powerful machines governed by software and AI. After all, computers and robots have no understanding of the harm that they might inadvertently inflict on humans.

The arrival of new technologies that take on human tasks could produce fear among employees, adding stress and frustration to the work environment and possibly exacerbating mental health issues. Organizations that once ignored employees' mental health are starting to assume more responsibility for this aspect of their employees' well-being.

Sustainability

Science is informing more sustainable working practices that diminish damage to our planet. Limiting energy consumption, greenhouse gas emissions, and waste, along with recycling and using renewable energy, have become standard practice. Organizations must protect their neighbors, the environment, and the planet, along with looking after their customers and employees.

IoT now provides real-time data to help leaders understand how their organization is impacting the environment and discover new ways to live up to their commitments. Data collection, number crunching, and reporting—as well as new methods of communication—can bring much-needed transparency and accountability.

Community

Community support demonstrates an organization's commitment to the stakeholders it serves. Where profit and efficiency were the prime drivers of the past, today's organizations understand that civic responsibility distinguishes them from the pack. Championing community initiatives, donating to charities, sponsoring the arts, conducting blood drives, backing support groups for underserved populations, and engaging with civic organizations all communicate an organization's desire to serve its community. So does creating an inclusive, accessible workplace where people feel appreciated and valued.

New Ways to Nurture and Inspire Talent

Top-down management and rigid annual evaluations are giving way to ongoing conversations, teamwork, collaboration, creative approaches to task management, and assessments that promote understanding. Tomorrow's jobs will demand strong skills in project management, task management, people management, and interpersonal communication, along with knowledge about specialized industry sectors and technology. From school districts to institutions of higher education, many educational organizations now recognize the need to shift from preparing students for a top-down world to cultivating skills that will help their graduates thrive in the coming years. Employers are making that shift too, and individuals who want to get ahead will strive for the needed skills and knowledge on their own.

As technology grows more complex and individuals become more specialized, they will need to collaborate in teams and direct their skillsets toward the team's completion of required tasks. To communicate well with their coworkers and collaborate effectively, individuals must develop emotional, social, and conversational intelligence along with technical skills. To facilitate this, organizations must embrace psychological safety, diversity, and inclusion and help people work effectively with machines as well as coworkers. The ability to provide real-time guidance as workers perform their tasks will boost their confidence as well as their performance. For longer-term skills development, employers have a host of new ways to evaluate current activities, identify desired new skills, and steer workers into appropriate learning experiences.

Diversity and Inclusion

Organizations innovate to get ahead and stay ahead. A workplace that values everyone's unique qualities and makes them feel included attracts talent and keeps workers engaged. Gathering input from teams of diverse people, whether on staff or as part of a crowdsourced project, yields ideas that can drive new business models, products, services, and solutions. Contributors to these efforts are more forthcoming and creative when they feel psychologically safe. They must be able to express their ideas freely and fully within a "speak-up" culture, confident that they can do so without damaging their reputations or careers. This freedom of working in a "speak-up" culture encourages people to suggest ideas that drive the organization forward. It also enables people to own their mistakes and learn from them in a respectful environment that welcomes fresh thinking. People with differing approaches to problem-solving, communication, and getting things done will sometimes disagree. However, organizations that highly value diversity and inclusion can preempt or mitigate friction by helping individuals develop the emotional, social, and communication skills that promote understanding.

Harmonious Relationships with Tech

Employees have long needed to work harmoniously with each other, but they now must develop good relationships with automation too. Artisans value their tools and form relationships with them, and this rapport is vital for their craft. People who partner with robots or other machines must cultivate the social and emotional intelligence needed to work effectively with them and respect their role. Evaluating personality traits, preferences, values, style, motives, and experience will help employers match humans with the right kinds of technologies.

Guide on the Side

Giving workers relevant on-the-spot information can help them improve their performance instantaneously. The ability of AI to respond to stimuli in real time makes it possible for a device to collect a request, match it up against what's possible, and indicate to the user that something is amiss. For example, a waiter equipped with a small tablet can receive feedback about a customer's request without running to the kitchen for advice. If a diner were to order a chicken sandwich without chicken, they would be ordering nothing more than two pieces of bread. The electronic guide on the side would tag this unusual request and prompt the waiter to double-check the customer's wishes.

Augmented Reality (AR) makes it possible to present data during a task, in the right place and at the right time, offering greater efficiency and, in some cases, safety. Imagine an autonomous delivery truck in Denver whose pilot is in Nashville or Omaha. The truck could drive along while drones take off from it to deliver parcels to people's doors. Sensors on the truck would show the pilot what's happening all around it. The pilot would see everything from battery status to weather conditions, and, yes, even the presence of people and birds. This comprehensive information, along with AI, would help the pilot determine when and where the truck and its drones can operate safely.

The New Skills Required

Predictive analytics and algorithms are helping employers to identify the new competencies required for particular jobs, improve job descriptions, and identify talented candidates. Innovative technology and new business practices demand complex problem-solving, critical thinking, strong leadership, clear communication, informed decision-making, and perceptive negotiation. Creativity, good judgment, persuasiveness, and flexibility are crucial too. Technical skills in demand relate to machine learning, data visualization, user-interface or user-experience design, cybersecurity, cloud computing, AI, data science, digital marketing, mobile application development, software testing, business analysis, natural language processing, industrial design, and blockchain-related technologies.

The Future of Learning

As the half-life of skills reduce and individuals and teams take on more creative roles to achieve organizational goals, learning experiences should become more flexible and individualized. When linked to job roles and competency models, online learning systems will provide pathways that help individuals develop the competencies they need to qualify for better jobs. Documentation of customized learning experiences will follow this pattern, offering portable credentials that reflect each person's unique path of learning and achievement.

Developing New Skills

Online learning systems have been evolving for decades and will continue to do so. At a primitive level, these systems are content dispensers and result trackers. But data analysis, machine learning, and AI will enable these systems to provide meaningful and insightful recommendations to help someone manage their education and career.

Education providers are using new technology tools to monitor learning progress—rather than seat time—toward a credential. They are customizing learning experiences to place individuals in those environments where they learn best and can focus more easily on content. These adjustments include even the time of day when an individual best absorbs information. As educational institutions become more intricately connected with industry, they will increasingly alter their programming to serve industry's growing need for competencies and micro-credentials.

Identifying the competencies needed for specific job roles will clear the way for employers to collaborate with educational institutions. For example, a hospital that needs to train staff members on the use of new equipment might approach the local community college to provide a three-week training module. Each learner's participation in that course will go onto their interoperable learning record (ILR) and remain accessible to them and their employers from then on. (ILRs are discussed in detail shortly.)

When learning and assessments need higher fidelity to simulate complex environments, we'll see more use of Virtual Reality (VR), which can help workers develop experience before they encounter issues in the real world. For instance, a sewer inspector could don VR glasses and learn, from what they see in multiple dimensions, what they will need to look for when they drop down into a utility hole. Is a wall in poor repair? Might it collapse? Now forewarned, the inspector will know what to expect and can plan for contingencies.

Credentials as a Currency

The need for lifelong learning in an ever-shifting employment landscape has brought competencies to the fore. An academic degree reflects someone's interest in a subject and possibly their preparation for a particular career. However, their skills and knowledge need to keep pace with dramatic changes in job roles and careers. To do so, they must pursue competencies in essential skills for their current or desired job.

With technology accelerating at breakneck rates and technical skills becoming more specialized, some university coursework might be out of date before the student graduates. All job seekers, including graduates, will need to develop new skills and submit proof of their achievements. Micro-credentials, supported by blockchain technology and digital badging, register competencies acquired through formal or informal learning experiences in the workplace or academic institutions.

Digital badges for each credential offer a verifiable way to document an individual's competencies, making it easy for job seekers to prove that their learning is up to date. Blockchain has made it possible to create digital ledgers of learning and qualifications that generate trustworthy, transparent credentials as an alternative to traditional transcripts and certificates.

Open Data Standards

Just as open data standards facilitate credit card processing anywhere in the world, they also provide a means of transferring data for competencies, learning, and content. For example, the International Organization for Standardization (ISO) published the ISO/IEC 20006 standard for dealing with competency information in Information Technology (IT) for learning, education, and training. The HR Open Standards Consortium provides a common vocabulary and data models to enable disparate HR systems to interoperate successfully. The SCORM (Sharable Content Object Reference Model) is a learning technology standard that determines how an e-learning course will be launched and tracked by a learning management system. Another specification, Experience API or XAPI, makes it possible to collect data about a wide range of experiences—everything from making a conference presentation to writing a thesis. The IMS Global Learning Consortium provides numerous standards for the academic community, including the Question and Test Interoperability specification, which eases the process of exchanging data about assessments.

National and international data standards

- enable systems, within different organizations, to transfer data, such as competency definitions, college transcripts, and certification easily;

- save software developers from reinventing the wheel;

- provide a vocabulary and framework for systems design and linkage; and

- allow clients to reference a standard for data export to prevent a vendor from holding data hostage.

Aligning Institutional, Workplace, and Individual Learning

Open data standards will align stakeholders, such as employers, educational institutions, and professional associations, by making it easy to exchange competency definitions among different systems.

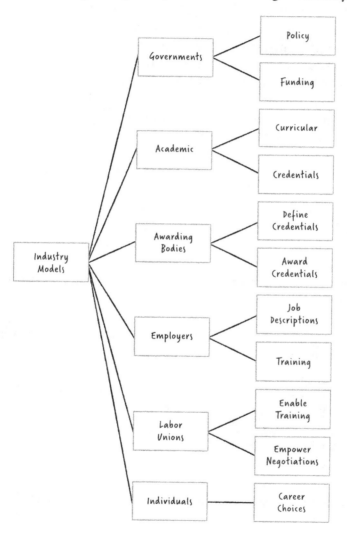

Figure 9.1: Uses of Competency Models

Government agencies and industry groups are developing open competency models to document future skills requirements. As illustrated in Figure 9.1, organizations can modify these models to meet their specific needs, use them within their training systems, relay them to educational institutions, and underpin certification programs. As an example, a college could train students in the competencies employers require. Current employees could learn the same competencies inhouse that students learn at the college. Micro-credentials would document everyone's achievement of those competencies, no matter who administered the coursework. By aligning with workplace needs, this granular approach to learning and recognition will allow individuals to target specific competencies without having to revisit material they have already learned.

Integrating Records of All Learning

Thanks to new open data standards, you will soon be able to integrate data garnered from an individual's coursework, training, assessments, and on-the-job activities. Also, personnel and HR systems will be able to track and analyze behaviors and sentiments, as well as learning experiences. Evaluating behaviors and capabilities together will help organizations design competency models that can more accurately predict job performance.

ILRs will be instrumental in tracking a wide variety of learning experiences, on-the-job behaviors, and more. ILRs will be able to document learning wherever it occurs—at work, through an educational program, or within military training. These records will be transferable and recognizable across academic, commercial, and military systems. Individuals seeking success in the new world of work will need this thorough reporting of their achievements. People who own and manage their individual learning history, mini-credentials, and competencies throughout their lives will have complete records of the learning experiences that have prepared them for their next step up.

The New World of Assessments

Assessments such as surveys, quizzes, and tests traditionally require a participant's full attention. But increasingly, organizations will be able to assess someone's competence through on-the-job data harvesting and analysis, with no need for the person to stop work. Both types of assessments potentially could help organizations diagnose learning needs, identify potential for higher responsibilities, and determine appropriate interventions. Data captured in the flow of work will enhance what employers learn from the results of traditional assessments by reflecting an individual's actual behaviors and performance on the job.

Enhancing Traditional Assessments

Surveys, quizzes, and tests will remain inexpensive and practical for use in training, certification, and credentialing. However, these reliable standbys will become increasingly

- accessible to people with limited sight, hearing, mobility, or other special needs, to provide a balanced, fair experience for everyone;

- available anywhere, on different devices, and at any time;

- authentic, simulating the workplace and using technology that participants will use on the job;

- correlated to job performance; and

- timely, providing quick, accurate results to the participant.

Other current and future trends for enhancing traditional assessments include the following:

- Use of assessment data to align learning experiences with an individual's needs.

- Regular assessments to strengthen memory recall and reinforce learning.

- Automated as well as human marking systems for response types that call for such tasks as essay writing, picture taking, and filming.

- Biometric authentication, such as fingerprint and facial recognition, for identification.

- Remote proctoring to allow individuals to take exams at home or work under controlled conditions.

- Enhanced use of data analysis to detect aberrant behaviors such as cheating.

- More observational assessments to provide evidence of an individual's behaviors and performance.

- Increased use of well-being assessments to evaluate employees' physical and mental health.

Real-time Data Collection

Amassing, analyzing, and correlating vast amounts of data from individuals' day-to-day interactions could help organizations evaluate how employees conduct themselves at work. For instance, software sensors installed on devices to track activities can yield data that can help organizations monitor worker efficiency, adherence to safety procedures, customer service, and more. Data analysis of employee's dealings with clients, and vendors can offer insights about sources of friction in organizational processes from customer acquisition to supply chain management. An added benefit of constant data collection and analysis is that workers or their supervisors can receive real-time prompts on how to improve performance.

Collecting data from daily activities at work has long-term and short-term value. For instance, it could help individuals and their coaches diagnose learning needs, spot emotional triggers, and identify potential for higher responsibilities. In the short term, data collected and analyzed in real time could make it possible to give an individual information and suggestions mid-task.

Data Collection Solutions

- Interconnected IoT devices that can report data directly to internal systems, which might conclude, for instance, that capacity decreased and error rates rose when an untrained person worked on the production line.

- Voice recognition and natural language processing that can prompt a customer service representative to ask more questions or offer a new product.

- People's sentiments harvested from text, pictures, and video cameras, which could alert supervisors to potential problems. For instance, if Jim is writing angry emails, natural language processing would flag a particularly harsh message and indicate the possible need for intervention. The next step would be to identify what's behind the anger: A subordinate's poor performance? Personal stress?

- Monitoring body language and facial expressions, which could indicate whether a person agrees or disagrees with a statement— or even whether they enjoy what they are doing. Sentiment analysis could become more critical as the ability of technology to monitor people's feelings improves.

- Technology that flags threatening or aberrant behavior, enabling a manager to forestall a physical attack by providing context for early intervention—perhaps something as simple as a conversation to determine what's behind the behavior.

- Organizations that monitor data in real time could alert a crane operator that the crane is off balance, warn of potential damage when a machine is working beyond its capacity, or instruct a truck driver to decelerate to stop excessive fuel usage.

Analyzing Data

Managers and coaches who use tools that correlate data harvested from assessments, machines, and devices will be able to

- identify skills gaps and direct individuals to the most appropriate learning experiences to develop the skills they lack;

- help leaders understand how individuals, teams, and organizations are transitioning to more fluid, responsive business models;

- prompt individuals to change their behavior when they are infracting organizational policies;

- confirm compliance with health, safety, and environmental policies and regulations;

- identify the need for new or replacement tools, and IA and robotics opportunities; and

- bring in new or external support or create new teams.

Like traditional assessments, data generated in the flow of work must be trustworthy. This data and its means of analysis must attain the same high standards of validity and reliability that testing and certification organizations have long required. The principles of measurement explained in Chapter 5 will still apply to the analysis of data collected from machines and devices. The aim is to derive defensible interpretations and conclusions from all sources of evidence.

Protecting Workers' Rights

Powerful tools can become weapons, so expect to hear deep concerns about how to balance talent transformation with the natural desire to guard people's privacy. Unions, workers' councils, privacy advocates, and security consultants need to champion practices that serve the common good. In many areas of the world, government regulations designed to protect workers' rights could sideline the tools and data that could benefit workers' professional development.

The tension between the right to privacy and the benefits of access to data will be debated for years to come.

Using the Talent Transformation Pyramid

As discussed in Chapter 3, dashboards based on the Talent Transformation Pyramid (p. 47) provide a holistic view of data from various sources within an organization. We've noted that although it's crucial to isolate each factor to measure it effectively, it's also essential to bring together all the information you've collected. Comprehensive data will bring patterns to light and expose correlations, making it easier to make well-informed decisions, predict readiness to perform, anticipate challenges, and determine appropriate interventions.

Traditional talent dashboards display information about recruitment, performance, succession, learning, certifications, and compensation. These dashboards will become increasingly dynamic and interactive. Future dashboards based on the pyramid will highlight correlations and provide drill-down capabilities to help leaders recognize the factor at the root of a problem. Having identified the source of an issue, they can then decide which interventions will be the most effective.

Keeping an eye on the pyramid's twelve factors and running analytics to reveal the interplay between them will position you to present helpful, meaningful, and persuasive metrics that promote understanding, cooperation, and progress. Using the pyramid as a framework for managing talent transformation, you will be ready to intervene at the right time, in the right place, with the right messages to help individuals, teams, and the entire organization improve performance.

Takeaways

- Blended technologies, new business models, a greater emphasis on social responsibility, and sophisticated approaches to talent management are driving change in the world of work.

- Lifelong learning, including the pursuit of competencies and credentials, will help people assume new roles and responsibilities.

- Technologies can now provide real-time data collection and analysis, including observations of an individual's actions, to augment data traditionally gathered from formal and informal learning experiences.

- Use the Talent Transformation Pyramid to see data from multiple sources and prompt appropriate interventions.

APPENDIX A

GLOSSARY OF TECHNOLOGIES

COMBINATIONS OF POWERFUL technologies are exponentially changing the world of work. Here, we explain some of the new technologies that, when blended, will accelerate progress during the Fourth Industrial Revolution.

Given that technology is growing exponentially we maintain an up-to-date list on our website at www.talenttransformation.com/book.

3D Printers

The ability to feed computer-aided design into a printer to produce a 3D object is a leading catalyst for industrial change. Creating proto-types easily and cheaply and manufacturing spare parts on demand are among 3D printing's many attractions; so are reduced just-in-case inventories, transportation costs, waste of raw materials, and carbon emissions. Flexibility is another—3D printers can process a growing range of materials, and they can add liquids or pow-dered materials layer by layer to produce strong, durable products. New machines, techniques, and materials available have enabled greater precision and repeatability, making 3D printing viable for large-scale production. No wonder many industries—including manufacturing, healthcare, architecture, defense, and education—are adapting this technology to their needs.

5G

The newest generation of wireless communications technologies supports cellular data networks. With greater speed, lower latency, and higher bandwidth than its predecessors, 5G will improve Virtual Reality (VR) and Augmented Reality (AR) experiences and revolu-tionize inter-vehicular communications and data collection and disbursement with geographically distributed devices. 5G could make in-home Internet connections unnecessary, just as cell phones have replaced traditional landline phones.

Artificial Intelligence (AI)

It is now possible for machines to learn and solve problems using neural networks that imitate the workings of the brain. AI enables a device to learn from data and adapt in a way that increases its ability to perform tasks. For example, chatbots can provide online customer service and improve their performance by learning from customer feedback.

There are several types of AI:

Narrow, Weak, or Basic AI

This form of AI focuses on a domain associated with a specific human ability. You could train a computer running narrow AI to beat a particular chess champion, but this does not necessarily mean that it would beat other chess champions. However, narrow AI can learn the rules of chess and play a version of itself to master the game. As another example, an AI system might be able to convert spoken words to text but not understand their meaning.

Artificial General Intelligence (AGI)

AGI will have far greater abilities than narrow AI. This technology will allow software to learn and perform tasks like a human. A machine running AGI will be able to learn new competencies and connect the dots across multiple domains. As AGI progresses, these machines will use visual, audio, and touch sensors to hear, listen, and see. These machines will be able to speak, move, interact with their environments, communicate with others, understand, reason, develop hypotheses, strategize, solve unfamiliar puzzles by trial and error, and make judgments with incomplete information.

Artificial Superintelligence (ASI)

ASI represents how machines might eventually become smarter than humans. ASI is appealing to some, but as it starts making independent decisions about the way we should live, it could pose a threat to life as we know it. Questions about the ethics of ASI include who can fine-tune or disable it if it starts working against the interests of the human race. Who will control these superintelligent machines? And how?

Augmented Reality (AR)

Digital augmentation of real-world environments adds useful data to what users see physically. Next time you watch a televised football game, you can thank AR for the lines drawn on the field to explain the plays. Unlike Virtual Reality (VR), described at the end of this section, AR provides information in the user's current physical context, so it does more than just simulate an environment. This capability makes it possible for AR to provide real-time support while employees perform tasks.

Bioprinting

Bioprinting, a form of 3D printing, is advancing quickly as a means of producing living tissue, bone, blood vessels, and, possibly, whole organs. Another potential use is for generating tissue for personalized treatment. The idea of human organ printing is exciting but raises ethical questions.

Blockchain

Blockchain enables trust between the parties in a transaction by providing a distributed ledger of transactions. This ledger, or database, lives simultaneously on multiple computers. Each new transaction, or block, added to the ledger includes a timestamp and a link to the previous block to form a chain. This decentralized structure allows users to manipulate information securely without losing the history of prior transactions. Blockchain has powered the development of cryptocurrency and, in the future, will be used to track micro-credentials.

Cloud Computing

Cloud computing makes online resources such as computing power, data storage, data replication, backup, operating systems, and applications available without requiring users to manage the underlying hardware and software. Typically, cloud computing resources occupy one or several data centers. Organizations can have exclusive access to a cloud or share it with others.

Organizations that use the cloud need not buy hardware or license software, which would require time and additional purchases to scale up the capacity. Instead, customers can connect to the cloud via "as-a-service" offerings and use just what they need: no more and no less. Here are some examples:

Infrastructure as a Service (IaaS)
IaaS provides a self-service model for accessing, monitoring, and managing data center infrastructures from a distance. Infrastructure includes computing resources (hardware or virtualized), storage, networking (including firewalls), and power.

Platform as a Service (PaaS)
In addition to delivering the same services at IaaS, PaaS provides and maintains the operating systems.

Software as a Service (SaaS)
In addition to providing the underlying platform and data maintenance, SaaS delivers applications for organizations and individuals to use, freeing customers from maintaining and upgrading them internally.

Machine Learning as a Service (MLaaS)
MLaaS is a subset of SaaS that allows users to use pre-configured algorithms and statistical models for fast and accurate pattern recognition.

Artificial Intelligence as a Service (AIaaS)
AIaaS is a subset of SaaS where clients can use pre-configured AI components for such things as natural language processing, voice recognition, and image recognition.

Data as a Service (DaaS)
DaaS provides access to data on demand. The service provider sources accurate data and pre-processes it to meet the client's needs.

Health Tech

New and blended technologies are transforming healthcare in many ways. For example:

- Machine Learning (ML) is exposing previously undetectable patterns of disease evidence.

- Artificial Intelligence (AI) can sort through numerous, complex options to recognize a disease, provide diagnosis, and suggest potential treatments.

- Massive computing power enables researchers to use genetic sequencing to identify at-risk groups and target personalized therapies to those most likely to benefit from them.

- 3D printers produce customized, low-cost prosthetics and medical devices.

- Organic material structures to replace kidneys, hearts, and even skin will follow.

- Computing and biotechnologies are creating new cancer treatments with less toxic side effects than current treatments.

- Devices embedded within clothing will continuously monitor vital signs. Also, enhanced biosensors will measure bodily functions, making it possible to get a meaningful, affordable, and rapid diagnosis via telemedicine.

- Natural language, image, and voice processing will analyze moods and emotions—and potentially prescribe Virtual Reality (VR) sessions to help change behaviors.

Internet of Things (IoT)

The interconnection of physical objects and digital communications enables everything from thermostats to cars to collect and share data in real time. The IoT allows you to warm up your house or turn on the lights when you are on your way home. Thanks to this merging of the physical and digital universe, everyday objects become "smart" objects. Data collected from smart devices might alert you to anomalies that need attention. As an example, with IoT monitoring pollen counts or pollution and with your device knowing your allergies, your device could alert you to conditions that might trigger a nasty reaction.

Machine Learning (ML)

ML systems can, given enough data, learn for themselves to categorize, sort, and find patterns of data that would be impossible to detect otherwise. As an example, ML makes it possible to categorize and identify objects, animals, and people easily. It also enables e-commerce websites to recommend products that pique your interest. If you have looked up similar products, the machine knows something about your needs and preferences. The more the machine "learns" about you, the more accurately it will lead you to products you want to buy, or people you'd like to meet.

Materials

Precisely engineered materials can be lightweight, durable, flexible, transparent, and absorbent. Or perhaps thin, easy to shape, and reusable. Materials engineering makes it possible to tailor the mix of these properties for next-generation products, including vehicles, solar power arrays, wind turbines, batteries, buildings, medical devices, protective gear, packaging, and biomedicine.

Robots

Robots perform specific tasks and carry out a complex series of actions. They come in all shapes and sizes and serve many different purposes. Here are several types:

Chatbots

Chatbots, now commonplace, provide meaningful interactions with customers when they contact banks, government agencies, airlines, and many other organizations. Developers who program chatbots used to guess at every path a conversation might take. But these days, AI-equipped chatbots use natural language processing and learn from previous conversational patterns to provide relevant help at the time of need. They offer convincing imitations of text or verbal conversations, but unlike their human counterparts, they can work 24/7. Chatbots are now deployed at scale to reduce the need for people in contact centers. Marketing, healthcare, and human resources teams are using more and more of these scalable, readily available digital helpers to engage in humanlike conversations to answer questions and concerns.

Collaborative Industrial Bots (Cobots)

Traditional robots work autonomously on mechanical tasks such as welding and spray painting. Workers do not go near them. Cobots, on the other hand, collaborate with humans. People provide intelligence and direction, and the cobots perform difficult, repetitive, or dangerous tasks. The cobots' safety features, manageable size, and ability to do a variety of tasks make them easy for people to use. Cobots can also improve efficiency. For instance, a cobot can take cues from a human's muscle tension to assist with an activity such as lifting a heavy object.

Delivery Robots

Autonomous robots, which have begun delivering packages, offer enormous commercial benefits to shipping companies. Now in their infancy, delivery bots will come in many configurations. Some will be heated and some refrigerated. Eventually, they might take off and land from automated trucks or fly from the warehouse directly to the customer's door. Cameras, speakers, microphones, 5G, and GPS will make it possible for delivery bots to provide safe, timely, and accurate service.

In-store Robots

In-store robots will interact with customers, answer questions, and find products. Using AI, a robot will recognize the customer, understand their voice, respond appropriately, simulate empathy when goods are not available, and provide useful options based on its knowledge of customer data.

Industrial Robots

Robots have been assembling physical products such as cars and smartphones with impressive dexterity for many years. The automotive industry, car parts manufacturers, and device assembly operations are the primary users of industrial robots for now. But as industrial robots become lighter, faster, and smarter, thanks to AI, they will learn how to perform increasingly sophisticated tasks.

Robotic Process Automation (RPA)

RPA uses software to automate business processes and complete repetitive tasks that employees might otherwise perform. RPA technologies eventually will use natural language processing and AI for such things as face and voice recognition. Current RPA tasks include screen-scraping unstructured information from websites and documents to insert into databases, processing paper invoices, completing expense claims, and producing proposals. Banks, insurance companies, and utilities are significant users of RPA, and more industries will follow suit as this technology matures.

Warehouse Robots

A variety of robots work in warehouses, and their numbers will continue to increase. Some of them lift heavy loads to stack racks, while more dexterous robots pick, pack, and ship products. Supply chain management data and consumer demand for immediate deliveries are driving organizations to make warehouse robots more autonomous and efficient.

Virtual Reality (VR)

Multidimensional, computer-generated replication simulates a physical space to create VR experiences. People currently interact with this environment by wearing a helmet equipped with a screen or gloves that have sensors in them. VR technologies will evolve to provide the same experience with less cumbersome hardware. Although VR is a popular form of entertainment, its simulation of real-world places and situations makes it invaluable in the workplace, especially as a means of helping individuals learn new skills.

APPENDIX B

ASSESSMENT TYPES AND THEIR USES

THE TABLE BELOW describes how to use various types of assessments. By "assessment," we mean any process in which evidence is judged, including tests and surveys. This table does not include clinical assessments that psychologists administer to diagnose and plan treatment for patients. A more comprehensive version of this table is available on the website at www.talenttran formation.com/book.

ASSESSMENT TYPES	DESCRIPTIONS
180-degree Assessments	Gather opinions about an individual from their colleagues and direct reports but not their boss
360-degree Assessments	Gather opinions about an individual from their coworkers, including their boss, peers, and direct reports
Ability Tests	Assess an individual's cognitive or physical abilities
Academic Entrance Tests	Evaluate suitability, in specific terms, for a particular educational opportunity

Attention Tests	Measure ability to focus, avoid distractions, and remain attentive
Certification Tests	Measure understanding of and ability to perform a variety of specific tasks
Course Evaluations	Collect opinions and levels of satisfaction with a course to improve the learning materials or the learning environment
Criterion-referenced Tests	Evaluate performance in relation to a pre-established benchmark
Diagnostic Assessments	Help determine appropriate and useful learning activities based on the gap between current skills and goals
Employee Net Promoter Scores (eNPS)	Measure the level of employee loyalty by asking, "What is the likelihood that you would recommend your employer to friend or colleague?"
Formative Assessments	Provide memory retrieval practice to strengthen recall
High-stakes Assessments	Deliver results that will have significant consequences for the test taker
Job Fit Tests	Ascertain values, preferences, motives, and personality traits to determine suitability for a specific job role
Job Task Analyses (JTA)	Identify the tasks required on the job or the behaviors and capabilities required to perform it
Level 1 Surveys as per the Kirkpatrick model	See course evaluations
Licensing Tests	Evaluate a candidate's understanding of and ability to perform the specific tasks required to obtain a government agency's license to work
Low-stakes Assessments	Deliver results with no consequences for the respondent
Mastery Tests	Demonstrate a high level of proficiency in a specific topic or topics
Medium-stakes Assessments	Deliver results that may have consequences for the test taker

Needs Analysis Surveys	Identify knowledge and skills gaps that exist within a team or organization, to inform course development or course administration
Needs Assessments	Identify the training needs for an individual, team, or organization
Net Promoter Scores (NPS)	Measure the level of satisfaction with a product, service, or organization
Objective Tests	Measure factual knowledge
Performance Tests	Measure ability to perform in real-world environments
Personality Tests	Ascertain values, preferences, motives, and personality traits
Placement Tests	Determine suitability for educational opportunities, potentially to provide placement recommendations
Post-course Tests	Measure knowledge and skills after a course to determine if participants have sufficiently learned the course material and, in some cases, are eligible to receive a certificate of completion
Pre-course Tests	Evaluate knowledge and skills before a course, to create intrigue among students, to inform the instructor of students' abilities, and to set a benchmark to see if any knowledge transfer occurred during the course
Pre-employment Tests	Ascertain suitability, in specific terms, for particular job roles
Quizzes	Provide formative assessments for individuals and offer evidence that they are or are not mastering the subject matter
Satisfaction Surveys	Measure levels of satisfaction with products or services
Screening Tests	Determine suitability, in broad terms, for specific job roles or educational opportunities
Selection Tests	Determine suitability, in specific terms, for particular job roles or educational opportunities
Self-assessments	Gather information from an individual to diagnose learning needs and make recommendations for further learning or development

Skills Gap Surveys	Identify knowledge and skills gaps that exist within a team or organization, to inform course development or course administration
Smile Sheets	*See* course evaluations
Speed Tests	Determine someone's ability to perform one or more tasks within a stated time
Strength Finders	Identify and often rank-order an individual's natural talents
Summative Assessments	Measure an individual's skills, knowledge, and abilities to determine if they are qualified to pass a course or achieve a qualification, credential, or micro-credential
Surveys	Collect and quantify opinions, habits, and behaviors
Team Fit Tests	Ascertain values, preferences, motives, and personality traits to determine suitability to work in a specific team

APPENDIX C

BIBLIOGRAPHY

Chapter 1: Transforming the Workplace

Bersin, Josh. "The Future of Work: It's Already Here ... And Not as Scary as You Think." *Josh Bersin*, September 21, 2016. https://joshbersin.com/staging2017/2016/09/the-future-of-work-its-already-here/.

Brown, Justin, Tom Gosling, Bhus Sethi, Blair Sheppard, Carol Stubbings, John Sviokla, Daria Zarubina, and Jon Williams. "Workforce of the Future: The Competing Forces Shaping 2030." PWC, 2018. https://www.pwc.com/gx/en/services/people-organisation/workforce-of-the-future/workforce-of-the-future-the-competing-forces-shaping-2030-pwc.pdf.

Bughin, Jacques, James Manyika, Jonathan Woetzel, and Frank Mattern. "A Future That Works: Automation, Employment, and Productivity." McKinsey Global Institute, January 2017.

Cann, Oliver. "Who Pays for the Reskilling Revolution? Investment to Safeguard America's At-Risk Workers Likely to Cost Government $29 Billion." World Economic Forum, January 22, 2019. https://www.weforum.org/press/2019/01/who-pays-for-the-reskilling-revolution-investment-to-safeguard-america-s-at-risk-workers-likely-to-cost-government-29-billion/.

Chainey, Ross. "This Is How COVID-19 Could Change the World of Work for Good." World Economic Forum, April 16, 2020.

https://www.weforum.org/agenda/2020/04/here-s-how-coronavirus-has-changed-the-world-of-work-covid19-adam-grant/.

Clifton, Donald O, and James K Harter. "Investing in Strengths." In *Positive Organizational Scholarship: Foundations of a New Discipline*, edited by Kim S Cameron, Jane E Dutton, and Robert E Quinn, 111–21. San Francisco, CA: Berrett-Kohler Publishers, 2003. https://strengthszone.com/wp-content/uploads/2016/01/Investing-In-Strengths.pdf.

Faina, Inês, and Filomena Almeida. "Key Competencies for Digital Transformation in Workplace." In *Knowledge, People, and Digital Transformation: Approaches for a Sustainable Future*, edited by Florinda Matos, Valter Vairinhos, Isabel Salavisa, Leif Edvinsson, and Maurizio Massaro, 219–34. Cham: Springer International Publishing, 2020. https://doi.org/10.1007/978-3-030-40390-4_14.

Finley, Dane. "Amazon and Microsoft Are Launching Initiatives to Accelerate Research and Treatments for the Coronavirus." *Business Insider*, March 24, 2020. https://www.businessinsider.com/amazon-microsoft-launch-coronavirus-research-initiatives-2020-3.

Gallup. "Gallup's Perspective on the Gig Economy and Alternative Work Arrangements." Gallup, 2018.

Haines, Jesse. "Free Virtual Digital Skills Training from Grow with Google." Google, May 11, 2020. https://www.blog.google/outreach-initiatives/grow-with-google/free-virtual-digital-skills-training-grow-google/.

Hancock, Bryan, Scott Rutherford, and Kate Lazaroff-Puck. "Getting Practical about the Future of Work." *The McKinsey Quarterly*. McKinsey & Company, Inc., 2020. https://www.mckinsey.com/business-functions/organization/our-insights/getting-practical-about-the-future-of-work.

Hanspal, Amar. "In the Age of Automation, Technology Will Be Essential to Reskilling the Workforce." World Economic Forum, March 6, 2020. https://www.weforum.org/agenda/2020/03/how-tech-can-lead-reskilling-in-the-age-of-automation/.

Harris, Briony. "Who Should Pay for Workers to Be Reskilled?" World Economic Forum, January 22, 2019. https://www.weforum.org/agenda/2019/01/who-should-pay-for-workers-to-be-reskilled-1/.

Irina, Kazmina, Lukyanov Pavel, Zhminko Nadezhda, Savchenko Inna, Yusupova Gulnara, and Zatsarinnaya Elena. "Fourth Industrial Revolution—Engineering Innovations for Labor Productivity Increasing." *Journal of Talent Development and Excellence* 12, no. 3s (April 22, 2020): 477–87.

Javaid, Mohd, Abid Haleem, Raju Vaishya, Shashi Bahl, Rajiv Suman, and Abhishek Vaish. "Industry 4.0 Technologies and Their Applications in Fighting COVID-19 Pandemic." *Diabetes Metab. Syndr.* 14, no. 4 (April 24, 2020): 419–22. https://doi.org/10.1016/j.dsx.2020.04.032.

Jesuthasan, Ravin, Tracey Malcolm, and Susan Cantrell. "How the Coronavirus Crisis Is Redefining Jobs." *Harvard Business Review*, April 22, 2020. https://hbr.org/2020/04/how-the-coronavirus-crisis-is-redefining-jobs.

Kurzweil, Ray. "The Law of Accelerating Returns." In *Alan Turing: Life and Legacy of a Great Thinker*, edited by Christof Teuscher, 381–416. Berlin: Springer Berlin Heidelberg, 2004. https://doi.org/10.1007/978-3-662-05642-4_16.

———. "The Law of Accelerating Returns." Kurzweil Accelerating Intelligence, March 7, 2001. https://www.kurzweilai.net/the-law-of-accelerating-returns.

Leaser, David. "IBM Launches New Professional Skills Program: The Top Five Soft Skills You Need to Succeed in Business." *IBM Training and Skills Blog*, April 25, 2019. https://www.ibm.com/blogs/ibm-training/ibm-releases-new-courses-the-top-five-soft-skills-you-need-to-succeed-in-business/.

Lee, Peter. "Bringing Together Deep Bioscience and AI to Help Patients Worldwide: Novartis and Microsoft Work to Reinvent Treatment Discovery and Development." *The Official Microsoft Blog*, October 1, 2019. https://blogs.microsoft.com/blog/2019/10/01/bringing-together-deep-bioscience-and-ai-to-help-patients-worldwide-novartis-and-microsoft-work-to-reinvent-treatment-discovery-and-development/.

Lloyds Banking Group. "Helping Britain Prosper: Annual Report and Accounts 2018." Lloyd's Banking Group, 2018. https://www.lloyds bankinggroup.com/globalassets/documents/investors/2018/2018_lbg_strategic_report.pdf.

Lund, Susan, James Manyika, Liz Hilton Segel, André Dua, Bryan Hancock, Scott Rutherford, and Brent Macon. "The Future of Work in America: People and Places, Today and Tomorrow." McKinsey Global Institute, July 2019. https://www.mckinsey.com/~/media/McKinsey/Featured%20Insights/Future%20of%20Organizations/The%20future%20of%20work%20in%20America%20People%20and%20places%20today%20and%20tomorrow/The-Future-of-Work-in-America-Full-Report.ashx.

Marr, Bernard. "Coronavirus: How Artificial Intelligence, Data Science and Technology Is Used to Fight the Pandemic." *Forbes*, March 13, 2020. https://www.forbes.com/sites/bernardmarr/2020/03/13/coronavirus-how-artificial-intelligence-data-science-and-technology-is-used-to-fight-the-pandemic/.

O'Donnell, Riia. "Accenture Says It Retrained 300K Workers in 4 Years." *HR Dive*, February 5, 2019. https://www.hrdive.com/news/accenture-says-it-retrained-300k-workers-in-4-years/547477/.

Pham, Quoc-Viet, Dinh C Nguyen, Won-Joo Hwang, and Pubudu N Pathirana. "Artificial Intelligence (AI) and Big Data for Coronavirus (COVID-19) Pandemic: A Survey on the State-of-the-Arts." *IEEE Transactions on Artificial Intelligence*, 2020. https://www.preprints.org/manuscript/202004.0383.

Popiel, Pawel. "'Boundaryless' in the Creative Economy: Assessing Free-lancing on Upwork." *Critical Studies in Media Communication* 34, no. 3 (2017): 220–33. https://doi.org/10.1080/15295036.2017.1282618.

PwC. "New World. New Skills. How to Start Upskilling." PwC. Accessed June 19, 2020. https://www.pwc.com/gx/en/issues/upskilling.html.

Radin, Jennifer, Steve Hatfield, Jeff Schwartz, and Colleen Bordeaux. "Closing the Employability Skills Gap." Deloitte, January 28, 2020. https://www2.deloitte.com/us/en/insights/focus/technology-and-the-future-of-work/closing-the-employability-skills-gap.html.

Sawers, Paul. "Amazon Commits $700 Million to 'Upskill' a Third of Its U.S. Workforce by 2025." *VentureBeat*, July 11, 2019. https://venturebeat.com/2019/07/11/amazon-commits-700-million-to-upskill-a-third-of-its-u-s-workforce-by-2025/.

Stefanova Ratcheva, Vesselina, and Till Leopold. "5 Things to Know about the Future of Jobs." World Economic Forum, 2018. https://www.weforum.org/agenda/2018/09/future-of-jobs-2018-things-to-know/.

"The Future of Jobs Report 2018." Insight Report. World Economic Forum, 2018. http://www3.weforum.org/docs/WEF_Future_of_Jobs_2018.pdf.

Van Durme, Yves, Brad Denny, Josh Bersin, Erica Volini, Jeff Schwartz, Indranil Roy, and Maren Hauptmann. "From Jobs to Superjobs : 2019 Global Human Capital Trends." Deloitte, April 11, 2019. https://www2.deloitte.com/us/en/insights/focus/human-capital-trends/2019/impact-of-ai-turning-jobs-into-superjobs.html.

Volini, Erica, Jeff Schwartz, Indra Roy, Maren Hauptmann, Yves Van Durme, Brad Denny, and Josh Bersin. "Leading the Social Enterprise: Reinvent with a Human Focus." Deloitte, 2019. https://www2.deloitte.com/content/dam/insights/us/articles/5136_HC-Trends-2019/DI_HC-Trends-2019.pdf.

Wellener, Paul, Ben Dollar, Heather Ashton Manolian, Luke Monck, and Aijaz Hussain. "The Future of Work in Manufacturing." Deloitte, April 13, 2020. https://www2.deloitte.com/us/en/insights/industry/manufacturing/future-of-work-manufacturing-jobs-in-digital-era.html.

World Economic Forum. "Fourth Industrial Revolution." World Economic Forum, September 2019. https://www.weforum.org/focus/fourth-industrial-revolution.

———. "The Future of Jobs: Employment, Skills and Workforce Strategy for the Fourth Industrial Revolution." World Economic Forum, January 2016. http://www3.weforum.org/docs/WEF_Future_of_Jobs.pdf.

World Economic Forum and Society Boston Consulting Group. "Towards a Reskilling Revolution: Industry-Led Action for the Future of Work." World Economic Forum, 2019. http://www3.weforum.org/docs/WEF_Towards_a_Reskilling_Revolution.pdf.

Zahidi, Saadia. "The Gig Economy Is Changing the Way We Work. Now Regulation Must Catch Up." World Economic Forum, June 28, 2016. https://www.weforum.org/agenda/2016/06/gig-economy-changing-work/.

Chapter 2: Embracing Change

Bravery, Kate. "Win with Empathy: Global Talent Trends Study 2020." Mercer, 2020. https://www.mercer.com/content/dam/mercer/attachments/private/global-talent-trends-2020-report.pdf.

Brynjolfsson, Erik, and Tom Mitchell. "What Can Machine Learning Do? Workforce Implications." *Science* 358, no. 6370 (December 22, 2017): 1530–34. https://doi.org/10.1126/science.aap8062.

Cameron, Esther, and Mike Green. *Making Sense of Change Management: A Complete Guide to the Models, Tools and Techniques of Organizational Change.* London; New York: Kogan Page Publishers, 2019.

De Smet, Aaron, Sébastien Lacroix, Angelika Reich, and Sapana Agrawal. "Beyond Hiring: How Companies Are Reskilling to Address Talent Gaps." McKinsey, February 12, 2020. https://www.mckinsey.com/business-functions/organization/our-insights/beyond-hiring-how-companies-are-reskilling-to-address-talent-gaps.

Dhiman, Satinder, and Joan Marques, eds. *New Horizons in Positive Leadership and Change: A Practical Guide for Workplace Transformation.* Cham, Switzerland: Springer, 2020. https://doi.org/10.1007/978-3-030-38129-5.

Goodman, Elisabeth, and Lucy Loh. "Organizational Change: A Critical Challenge for Team Effectiveness." *Business Information Review* 28, no. 4 (December 1, 2011): 242–50. https://doi.org/10.1177/0266382111427087.

Hodges, Julie. *Managing and Leading People through Organizational Change: The Theory and Practice of Sustaining Change through People.* London: Kogan Page Publishers, 2016.

Hupfer, Susanne. "Talent and Workforce Effects in the Age of AI: Insights from Deloitte's State of AI in the Enterprise." Deloitte, 2020. https://www2.deloitte.com/content/dam/insights/us/articles/6546_talent-and-workforce-effects-in-the-age-of-ai/DI_Talent-and-workforce-effects-in-the-age-of-AI.pdf.

Kübler-Ross, Elisabeth, and David Kessler. *On Grief and Grieving: Finding the Meaning of Grief through the Five Stages of Loss.* New York: Simon and Schuster, 2014.

Kurzweil, Ray. "The Law of Accelerating Returns." Kurzweil Accelerating Intelligence, March 7, 2001. https://www.kurzweilai.net/the-law-of-accelerating-returns.

Lauby, Sharlyn. "How to Create a Recruiting Strategy: Buy, Build, and Borrow." SHRM, November 5, 2018. https://www.shrm.org/resourcesandtools/hr-topics/talent-acquisition/pages/how-to-create-a-recruiting-strategy.aspx.

Lewin, Kurt. *The Conceptual Representation and the Measurement of Psychological Forces*, 1938 reprint edition. Martino Fine Books, 2013.

Manyika, James, Susan Lund, Michael Chui, Jacques Bughin, Jonathan Woetzel, Parul Batra, Ryan Ko, and Saurabh Sanghvi. "Jobs Lost, Jobs Gained: Workforce Transitions in a Time of Automation." McKinsey Global Institute, 2017. https://www.mckinsey.com/~/media/mckinsey/featured%20insights/Future%20of%20Organizations/What%20the%20future%20of%20work%20will%20mean%20for%20jobs%20skills%20and%20wages/MGI-Jobs-Lost-Jobs-Gained-Report-December-6-2017.ashx.

Narayanasamy, N. "Force Field Analysis." In *Participatory Rural Appraisal: Principles, Methods and Application*, edited by N Narayanasamy, 247–58. New Delhi: Sage, 2009.

Quatrale, Shelley. "Resistance to Organizational Change: Causes, Attitudes, and Mitigations," 2015. http://www.academia.edu/download/53154266/Resistance_to_Change__Causes__Attitudes_and_Mitigations.pdf.

Quindazzi, Mike. "Artificial Intelligence and the Role of Workers." Samsung, May 4, 2017. https://insights.samsung.com/2017/05/04/artificial-intelligence-and-the-role-of-workers/.

Rouw, Anne Laure. "How to Amplify Your Smart Workforce with Robotics." Accenture, September 11, 2017. https://www.accenture.com/nl-en/blogs/insights/how-to-amplify-your-smart-workforce-with-robotics.

Schwab, Klaus. "The Fourth Industrial Revolution: What It Means, How to Respond." *Foreign Affairs*, December 12, 2015.

Taulli, Tom. *The Robotic Process Automation Handbook: A Guide to Implementing RPA Systems*. Berkeley, CA: Apress, 2020.

Young, Mary B. "Buy, Build, Borrow, or None of the Above? New Options for Closing Global Talent Gaps." The Conference Board, 2015. http://www.cewd.org/documents/BuyBuildBorrow-ConferenceBoard.pdf.

Chapter 3: A Holistic Framework: The Talent Transformation Pyramid

Bonesso, Sara, Elena Bruni, and Fabrizio Gerli. "Emotional and Social Intelligence Competencies in the Digital Era." In *Behavioral Competencies of Digital Professionals: Understanding the Role of Emotional Intelligence*, edited by Sara Bonesso, Elena Bruni, and Fabrizio Gerli, 41–62. Cham: Springer International Publishing, 2020. https://doi.org/10.1007/978-3-030-33578-6_3.

Brackett, Marc A, Susan E Rivers, and Peter Salovey. "Emotional Intelligence: Implications for Personal, Social, Academic, and Workplace Success." *Soc. Personal. Psychol. Compass* 5, no. 1 (January 4, 2011): 88–103. https://doi.org/10.1111/j.1751-9004.2010.00334.x.

Caplan, Janice. *Strategic Talent Development: Develop and Engage All Your People for Business Success*. London: Kogan Page Publishers, 2013.

Carmeli, Abraham. "The Relationship between Emotional Intelligence and Work Attitudes, Behavior and Outcomes." *Journal of Managerial Psychology* 18, no. 8 (2003): 788–813. https://doi.org/10.1108/02683940310511881.

Carmeli, Abraham, and Zvi E Josman. "The Relationship among Emotional Intelligence, Task Performance, and Organizational Citizenship Behaviors." *Hum. Perform.* 19, no. 4 (October 1, 2006): 403–19. https://doi.org/10.1207/s15327043hup1904_5.

Cascio, Wayne F, and Herman Aguinis. *Applied Psychology in Talent Management*. Los Angeles: SAGE Publications, 2018.

Christenko, Aleksandr, Žilvinas Martinaitis, and Simonas Gaušas. "Specific and General Skills: Concepts, Dimensions, and Measurements." *Competition & Change* 24, no. 1 (January 1, 2020): 44–69. https://doi.org/10.1177/1024529419882554.

Christian, Michael S, Jill C Bradley, J Craig Wallace, and Michael J Burke. "Workplace Safety: A Meta-analysis of the Roles of Person and Situation

Factors." *J. Appl. Psychol.* 94, no. 5 (September 2009): 1103–27. https://doi.org/10.1037/a0016172.

Cole, Kris. *Leadership and Management: Theory and Practice.* Victoria, Australia: Cengage, 2018.

Deming, David J. "The Growing Importance of Social Skills in the Labor Market." *Q. J. Econ.* 132, no. 4 (2017): 1593–1640.

Finger, Matthias. "From Knowledge to Action? Exploring the Relationships between Environmental Experiences, Learning, and Behavior." *J. Soc. Issues* 50, no. 3 (October 1994): 141–60. https://doi.org/10.1111/j.1540-4560.1994.tb02424.x.

Hauff, Sven, and Stefan Kirchner. "Changes in Workplace Situation and Work Values. Relations and Dynamics within Different Employment Regimes." *Management Revue* 25, no. 1 (2014): 27–49.

Kassel, Kerul, Isabel Rimanoczy, and Shelley F Mitchell. "The Sustainable Mindset: Connecting Being, Thinking, and Doing in Management Education," *Acad. Man. Ann. Proc.* 1 (2016): 16659. https://journals.aom.org/doi/abs/10.5465/ambpp.2016.16659abstract.

Kerzner, Harold. *Project Management: A Systems Approach to Planning, Scheduling, and Controlling.* New Jersey: John Wiley & Sons, 2017.

Lencioni, Patrick. *The Five Dysfunctions of a Team.* New Jersey: John Wiley & Sons, 2006. http://dschoenherr.fatcow.com/sitebuildercontent/sitebuilderfiles/the_five_dysfunctions_of_a_team.pdf.

Oswald, Fred, Tara S Behrend, and Lori Foster. *Workforce Readiness and the Future of Work.* London: Routledge, 2019.

Pelster, Bill, Dani Johnson, Jen Stempel, and Bernard van der Vyver. "Careers and Learning: Real Time, All the Time: 2017 Global Human Capital Trends." Deloitte, February 28, 2017. https://www2.deloitte.com/us/en/insights/focus/human-capital-trends/2017/learning-in-the-digital-age.html.

Prada, María Fernanda, and Graciana Rucci. "Guide to Workforce Skills Assessment Instruments." IDB-TN-1070. Inter-American Development Bank, June 2016. https://publications.iadb.org/publications/english/document/Guide-to-Workforce-Skills-Assessment-Instruments.pdf.

Rumsey, Michael G. "Personality and Interests for Selection: Theoretical Perspectives." *Mil. Psychol.* 32, no. 1 (January 2, 2020): 7–23. https://doi.org/10.1080/08995605.2019.1652478.

Savitz, Andrew. *Talent, Transformation, and the Triple Bottom Line: How Companies Can Leverage Human Resources to Achieve Sustainable Growth.* New Jersey: John Wiley & Sons, 2013.

Schmitt, Neal. *The Oxford Handbook of Personnel Assessment and Selection.* New York: Oxford University Press, 2012.

Turner, Paul. "The Psychology of Work and Employee Engagement." In *Employee Engagement in Contemporary Organizations: Maintaining High Productivity and Sustained Competitiveness*, edited by Paul Turner, 113–40. Cham, Switzerland: Springer International Publishing, 2020. https://doi.org/10.1007/978-3-030-36387-1_5.

Chapter 4: Assessments—Past, Present, and Future

AIHR. "About Us: We Are AIHR." Accessed June 19, 2020. https://www.aihr.com/about-us/.

Bauer, Talya N. "Onboarding New Employees: Maximizing Success." SHRM, 2010. https://www.shrm.org/hr-today/trends-and-forecasting/special-reports-and-expert-views/Documents/Onboarding-New-Employees.pdf.

Burke, Eugene, and John Kleeman. "Assessing for Situational Judgment: Designing, Deploying and Getting Value from Situational Judgment Assessments." White Paper. Questionmark, 2018.

Crotts, Katrina, Stephen G Sireci, and April Zenisky. "Evaluating the Content Validity of Multistage-adaptive Tests." *Journal of Applied Testing Technology* 13, no. 1 (April 1, 2012). http://www.jattjournal.com/index.php/atp/article/view/48368.

Deaux, Kay, and Mark Snyder, eds. *The Oxford Handbook of Personality and Social Psychology.* New York: Oxford University Press, 2018.

Gallup. "Re-Engineering Performance Management." Gallup, January 8, 2018. https://www.gallup.com/workplace/238064/re-engineering-performance-management.aspx.

Goldstein, Harold W, Elaine D Pulakos, Carla Semedo, and Jonathan Passmore, eds. *The Wiley Blackwell Handbook of the Psychology of Recruitment, Selection and Employee Retention.* New Jersey: John Wiley & Sons, 2017.

Jacobucci, Ross, and Kevin J Grimm. "Machine Learning and Psychological Research: The Unexplored Effect of Measurement." *Perspect. Psychol. Sci.*, April 29, 2020, 1745691620902467. https://doi.org/10.1177/1745691620902467.

James, William. *Principles of Psychology*. New York: Henry Holt and Company, 1890.

John, Oliver P, Richard W Robins, and Lawrence A Pervin, eds. *Handbook of Personality: Theory and Research*. 3rd edition. New York: Guilford Press, 2008.

Jones, Thomas O, and W Earl Sasser. "Why Satisfied Customers Defect." *Harvard Business Review*, November 1, 1995. https://hbr.org/1995/11/why-satisfied-customers-defect.

Marr, Bernard. "Marketing KPIs: How To Measure Customer Engagement." *Bernard Marr*. Accessed June 19, 2020. https://www.bernardmarr.com/default.asp?contentID=1375.

Muchinsky, Paul M. *Psychology Applied to Work: An Introduction to Industrial and Organizational Psychology*. 12th edition. Summerfield, NC: Hypergraphic Press, 2019.

PeopleMetrics. "Customer Engagement vs. Customer Satisfaction." PeopleMetrics, September 30, 2010. https://www.peoplemetrics.com/blog/customer-engagement-vs-customer-satisfaction-which-should-you-follow.

Raad, Boele de, and Marco Perugini, eds. "Big Five Factor Assessment: Introduction." In *Big Five Assessment*, edited by Boele de Raad and Marco Perugini, 1–18. Boston: Hogrefe & Huber Publishers, 2002.

Salgado, Jesus F. "The Five Factor Model of Personality and Job Performance in the European Community." *J. Appl. Psychol.* 82, no. 1 (February 1997): 30–43. https://doi.org/10.1037/0021-9010.82.1.30.

Saloni, Jadhav, Jaras Mansi, Patil Payal, and Sonawane Sunita. "Survey on Personality Predication Methods Using AI." *International Journal of Advanced Engineering, Management and Science (IJAEMS)* 5, no. 12 (2019): 656–58.

Sheeba, M Jyothi, and Prabu B Christopher. "Exploring the Role of Training and Development in Creating Innovative Work Behaviors and Accomplishing Non-routine Cognitive Jobs for Organizational

Effectiveness." *J. Toxicol. Environ. Health B Crit. Rev.* 7, no. 4 (2019): 2020.

Shields, John. *Managing Employee Performance and Reward: Concepts, Practices, Strategies.* UK: Cambridge University Press, 2007.

Skok, David. "Measure Customer Engagement: Increase Conversion and Lower Churn." For Entrepreneurs, September 19, 2011. https://www. forentrepreneurs.com/customer-engagement/.

Thomas, Jay C, ed. *Comprehensive Handbook of Psychological Assessment, Volume 4: Industrial and Organizational Assessment.* Hoboken, N.J: John Wiley & Sons, 2003.

Truxillo, Donald M, Talya N Bauer, and Berrin Erdogan. *Psychology and Work: Perspectives on Industrial and Organizational Psychology.* New York; London: Routledge, 2015.

Turner, Caroline, and Belinda Board. "A Critical Review of the Measurement of Potential Risk-posing Personality Traits and Their Application in the Workplace." In *Corporate Psychopathy: Investigating Destructive Personalities in the Workplace,* edited by Katarina Fritzon, Nathan Brooks, and Simon Croom, 173–98. Cham: Springer International Publishing, 2020. https://doi. org/10.1007/978-3-030-27188-6_6.

Victoria State Government. "Best Practice Guide: Recruitment and Selection." Victoria State Government, February 10, 2020. https:// www.education.vic.gov.au/hrweb/Documents/Best-Practice-Guide-Recruitment-Selection.pdf.

Vulpen, Erik van. "21 HR Data Sources for Analytics." AIHR Analytics, March 2, 2020. https://www.analyticsinhr.com/blog/hr-data-sources/.

Woods, Stephen A, Sara Ahmed, Ioannis Nikolaou, Ana Cristina Costa, and Neil R Anderson. "Personnel Selection in the Digital Age: A Review of Validity and Applicant Reactions, and Future Research Challenges." *Eur. J. Work Org. Psychol.* 29, no. 1 (January 2, 2020): 64–77. https://doi.org/1 0.1080/1359432X.2019.1681401.

Work Learning Research. "Smile Sheets." Accessed June 19, 2020. https:// www.worklearning.com/smilesheets/.

Zeigler-Hill, Virgil, and Todd K Shackelford, eds. *The SAGE Handbook of Personality and Individual Differences: Volume III: Applications of Personality and Individual Differences.* Los Angeles: SAGE, 2018.

Chapter 5: Principles of Measurement

Brannick, Michael T, Eduardo Salas, and Carolyn W Prince, eds. *Team Performance Assessment and Measurement: Theory, Methods, and Applications*. New York: Psychology Press, 1997.

Church, Allan H, and Christopher T Rotolo. "How Are Top Companies Assessing Their High-potentials and Senior Executives? A Talent Management Benchmark Study." *Consulting Psychology Journal: Practice and Research* 65, no. 3 (September 2013): 199–223. https://doi. org/10.1037/a0034381.

"Classical Test Theory—an Overview." ScienceDirect. Accessed May 9, 2020. https://www.sciencedirect.com/topics/computer-science/classical-test-theory.

"Concurrent Validity—an Overview." ScienceDirect. Accessed June 20, 2020. https://www.sciencedirect.com/topics/psychology/concurrent-validity.

Coulacoglou, Carina, and Donald H Saklofske. *Psychometrics and Psychological Assessment: Principles and Applications*. Academic Press, 2017.

Delves, Don, Amy DeVylder Levanat, and John M Bremen. "Human Capital Governance: The Beginning of a New Era." Willis Tower Watson, March 27, 2020. https://www.willistowerswatson.com/en-US/Insights/2020/03/human-capital-governance-the-beginning-of-a-new-era.

Haynes, Stephen N, David C S Richard, and Edward S Kubany. "Content Validity in Psychological Assessment: A Functional Approach to Concepts and Methods." *Psychol. Assess.* 7, no. 3 (1995): 238–47.

"Item Characteristic Curve—an Overview." ScienceDirect. Accessed May 9, 2020. https://www.sciencedirect.com/topics/psychology/item-characteristic-curve.

Kaplan, Robert M, and Dennis P Saccuzzo. *Psychological Testing: Principles, Applications, and Issues*. Cengage Learning, 2012.

Kleeman, John, and Eric Shepherd. "Assessment Results You Can Trust." White Paper. Questionmark, 2015.

Kline, Theresa. "Classical Test Theory: Assumptions, Equations, Limitations, and Item Analyses." In *Psychological Testing: A Practical*

Approach to Design and Evaluation, 91–106. Thousand Oaks, CA: SAGE, 2005. https://methods.sagepub.com/base/download/BookChapter/psychological-testing/n5.xml.

Ones, Deniz S, Chockalingam Viswesvaran, and Frank L Schmidt. "No New Terrain: Reliability and Construct Validity of Job Performance Ratings." *Ind. Organ. Psychol.* 1, no. 2 (June 2008): 174–79. https://doi.org/10.1111/j.1754-9434.2008.00033.x.

Robins, Richard W, R Chris Fraley, and Robert F Krueger, eds. *Handbook of Research Methods in Personality Psychology*. New York; London: Guilford Press, 2009.

Rockwood, Kate. "Assessing Personalities." SHRM, February 29, 2020. https://www.shrm.org/hr-today/news/all-things-work/pages/personality-assessments.aspx.

Rohrer, Julia M. "Thinking Clearly about Correlations and Causation: Graphical Causal Models for Observational Data." *Advances in Methods and Practices in Psychological Science* 1, no. 1 (March 1, 2018): 27–42. https://doi.org/10.1177/2515245917745629.

Shrock, Sharon A, and William C Coscarelli. *Criterion-referenced Test Development: Technical and Legal Guidelines for Corporate Training*. 3rd edition. New Jersey: John Wiley & Sons, 2008.

Sørlie, Henrik O, Jørn Hetland, Anders Dysvik, Thomas H Fosse, and Øyvind L Martinsen. "Person-Organization Fit in a Military Selection Context." *Mil. Psychol.* 32, no. 3 (May 3, 2020): 237–46. https://doi.org/10.1080/08995605.2020.1724752.

Wainer, Howard, and David Thissen. "True Score Theory: The Traditional Method." In *Test Scoring*, edited by David Thissen and Howard Wainer, 422:23–72. Mahwah, NJ: Lawrence Erlbaum Associates Publishers, 2001. https://psycnet.apa.org/fulltext/2001-01226-001.pdf.

Westgaard, Odin. *Tests That Work: Designing and Delivering Fair and Practical Measurement Tools in the Workplace*. New Jersey: John Wiley & Sons, 1999.

Wright, Patrick M, Timothy M Gardner, Lisa M Moynihan, Hyeon Jeong Park, Barry Gerhart, and John E Delery. "Measurement Error in Research on Human Resources and Firm Performance: Additional Data and Suggestions for Future Research." *Personnel Psychology* 54, no. 4 (2001): 875–901.

Chapter 6: Assessing Individuals

c8 Sciences. "Multiple Simultaneous Attention." c8 Sciences. Accessed June 20, 2020. https://www.c8sciences.com/about/8ccc/multiple-simultaneous-attention/.

Carpenter, Heather, and Tera Qualls. *The Talent Development Platform: Putting People First in Social Change Organizations*. San Francisco, CA: John Wiley & Sons, 2015.

"Competency Model." Training Industry, May 23, 2013. https://trainingindustry.com/wiki/professional-development/competency-model/.

Crotts, Katrina, Stephen G Sireci, and April Zenisky. "Evaluating the Content Validity of Multistage-adaptive Tests." *Journal of Applied Testing Technology* 13, no. 1 (April 1, 2012). http://www.jattjournal.com/index.php/atp/article/view/48368.

Dick, Walter, and Nancy Hagerty. *Topics in Measurement: Reliability and Validity*. New York: McGraw-Hill, 1971.

Ennis, Susan. "Assessing Employee Competencies." In *Evaluating Corporate Training: Models and Issues*, edited by Stephen M Brown and Constance J Seidner, 183–208. Dordrecht: Springer Netherlands, 1998. https://doi.org/10.1007/978-94-011-4850-4_9.

Fehriinger, Heather M. "Contributions and Limitations of Cattell's Sixteen Personality Factor Model." *Trabajo de Investigacion En Linea Citado El* 3 (2004). http://www.personalityresearch.org/papers/fehringer.html.

Gallup. "Gallup's Perspective on Creating an Exceptional Onboarding Journey for New Employees." Gallup, 2019.

IHRDC. "Linking Competencies with an Integrated Talent Management Philosophy." IHRDC, February 2014. https://www.ihrdc.com/pdfs/IHRDC-Linking-Competencies-with-Integrated-Talent-Management-Philosophy.pdf.

Kirkpatrick, Donald, and James Kirkpatrick. *Evaluating Training Programs: The Four Levels*. San Francisco: Berrett-Koehler Publishers, 2006.

Kleeman, John, and Eric Shepherd. "The Role of Assessments in Mitigating Risk for Financial Services Organizations: Good Practice in Using Questionmark Assessments for Regulatory Compliance." White Paper. Questionmark, 2020.

Luenendonk, Martin. "How to Organize and Run an Assessment Center." Cleverism, August 22, 2015. http://cleverism.com/how-to-organize-and-run-assessment-center/.

Merrick, Caren. "Six Benefits to Knowing Your Value & Strengths—Here's How." Caren Merrick, March 12, 2015. https://carenmerrick.com/six-benefits-knowing-value-strengths-heres/.

Povah, Nigel, and George C III Thornton, eds. *Assessment Centres and Global Talent Management*. London: Routledge, 2011.

Rath, Tom. *StrengthsFinder 2.0*. Gallup Press, 2007.

Shepherd, Eric, and Janet Godwin. "Assessments through the Learning Process." White Paper. Questionmark, 2004. https://www.questionmark.com/resources/whitepapers/.

Shields, John, Jim Rooney, Michelle Brown, and Sarah Kaine. "Performance Appraisal and Management." In *Managing Employee Performance and Reward: Systems, Practices and Prospects*, 3rd ed., 94–151. Cambridge: Cambridge University Press, 2020. https://www.cambridge.org/core/books/managing-employee-performance-and-reward/performance-appraisal-and-management/C8CCDEC4 2017BC0FD56AA3292702CB5C.

"What Are Assessment Centers?" Developmental Associates. Accessed June 20, 2020. https://www.developmentalassociates.com/client-openings/what-are-assessment-centers/.

Wigert, Ben, and Jim Harter. "Re-engineering Performance Management." Gallup, 2017. https://www.gallup.com/file/workplace/238064/Re-EngineeringPerformanceManagement_2018.pdf.

Chapter 7: Assessing Teams

Belbin, Meredith. "The Nine Belbin Team Roles," 2020. https://www.belbin.com/about/belbin-team-roles/.

Bergeron, Natasha, Aaron De Smet, and Liesje Meijknecht. "Improve Your Leadership Team's Effectiveness through Key Behaviors," January 27, 2020. https://www.mckinsey.com/business-functions/organization/our-insights/the-organization-blog/improve-your-leadership-teams-effectiveness-through-key-behaviors.

Bonebright, Denise A. "40 Years of Storming: A Historical Review of Tuckman's Model of Small Group Development." *Human Resource Development International* 13, no. 1 (February 1, 2010): 111–20. https://doi.org/10.1080/13678861003589099.

"Developing and Sustaining High-Performance Work Teams." SHRM. Accessed May 7, 2020. https://www.shrm.org/resourcesandtools/tools-and-samples/toolkits/pages/developingandsustaininghigh-performanceworkteams.aspx.

Ferrazzi, Keith. "Getting Virtual Teams Right." *Harvard Business Review*, December 1, 2014. https://hbr.org/2014/12/getting-virtual-teams-right.

Fulk, H Kevin, Reginald L Bell, and Nancy Bodie. "Team Management by Objectives: Enhancing Developing Teams' Performance." *Journal of Management Policy and Practice* 12, no. 3 (2011): 17–26.

Gallup. "How to Improve Teamwork in the Workplace." Gallup, 2020. https://www.gallup.com/cliftonstrengths/en/278225/how-to-improve-teamwork.aspx.

Hackman, J Richard, Ruth Wageman, and Colin M Fisher. "Leading Teams When the Time Is Right: Finding the Best Moments to Act." *Organ. Dyn.*, 2009. https://dash.harvard.edu/bitstream/handle/1/4412633/SD+Hackman+Leading+Teams.pdf?sequence=1.

Halverson, Claire B. "Group Process and Meetings." In *Effective Multicultural Teams: Theory and Practice*, edited by Claire B Halverson and S Aqeel Tirmizi, 111–33. Dordrecht: Springer Netherlands, 2008. https://doi.org/10.1007/978-1-4020-6957-4_5.

Haughey, Duncan. "RACI Matrix." Project Smart, 2017. https://www.projectsmart.co.uk/raci-matrix.php.

Jacka, J Mike, and Paulette J Keller. "RACI Matrices." In *Business Process Mapping*, edited by J Mike Jacka and Paulette J Keller, 255–75. New Jersey: John Wiley & Sons, Inc., 2012. https://doi.org/10.1002/9781119198390.ch10.

Kozlowski, Steve W J, and Bradford S Bell. "Work Groups and Teams in Organizations." In *Handbook of Psychology (Vol. 12): Industrial and Organizational Psychology*, edited by W C Borman, D R Ilgen, and R J Klimoski, 333–75. New York: Wiley-Blackwell, 2003.

Kozlowski, Steve W J, and Daniel R Ilgen. "Enhancing the Effectiveness of Work Groups and Teams." *Psychol. Sci. Public Interest* 7, no. 3 (December 2006): 77–124. https://doi.org/10.1111/j.1529-1006.2006.00030.x.

Lamson, Melissa. "Best Practices for Managing Dispersed Teams." *Inc.*, April 11, 2018. https://www.inc.com/melissa-lamson/3-strategies-to-successfully-lead-virtual-teams.html.

Li, Lori. "20+ Team-Building Activities to Build Trust Among Coworkers." Tinypulse, June 1, 2020. https://www.tinypulse.com/blog/team-building-activity-trust.

Liu, Mengqiao, Jason L Huang, and Marcus W Dickson. "Team Assessment and Selection." In *The Wiley Blackwell Handbook of the Psychology of Recruitment, Selection and Employee Retention*, edited by Harold W Goldstein, Elaine D Pulakos, Jonathan Passmore, and Carla Semedo, 310–33. Basingstoke, UK: Wiley, 2017. https://doi.org/10.1002/9781118972472.ch15.

Luecke, Richard. *Creating Teams with an Edge: The Complete Skill Set to Build Powerful and Influential Teams*. Boston: Harvard Business School Press, 2004.

McDaniel, Susan, Eduardo Salas, and Anne Kazak. "The Science of Teamwork." *American Psychologist* 73, no. 4 (June 2018). https://www.apa.org/pubs/journals/special/4017305.

Mulder, Patty. "Benne and Sheats Group Roles: 26 Powerful Group Roles." Toolshero, March 22, 2019. https://www.toolshero.com/leadership/benne-sheats-group-roles/.

Murphy, John J. *Pulling Together: 10 Rules for High Performance Teamwork*. Naperville, IL: Simple Truths, 2016.

Myers, Scott A, and Carolyn M Anderson. *The Fundamentals of Small Group Communication*. California: SAGE, 2008.

Neeley, Tsedal. "Global Teams That Work." *Harvard Business Review*, October 1, 2015.

Pulakos, Elaine Diane. *Selection Assessment Methods: A Guide to Implementing Formal Assessments to Build a High-quality Workforce*. Alexandria, VA: SHRM Foundations, 2005.

Richard Hackman, J, and Richard J Hackman. *Leading Teams: Setting the Stage for Great Performances*. Boston: Harvard Business Press, 2002.

Ross, Peggy. "RACI Matrix." University of Washington, August 22, 2019. https://wiki.cac.washington.edu/display/TEGPM/RACI+Matrix.

"Six Thinking Hats." de Bono Group. Accessed June 20, 2020. http://www.debonogroup.com/six_thinking_hats.php.

Stein, Judith. "Using the Stages of Team Development." MIT. Accessed May 7, 2020. https://hr.mit.edu/learning-topics/teams/articles/stages-development.

Sussman, Jesse. "55 Fun Virtual Team Building Activities for Remote Teams." Museum Hack, June 15, 2020. https://museumhack.com/virtual-team-building-for-remote-teams/.

"Team Trust Assessment." Teamwork Principals, May 14, 2019. https://teamworkprincipals.com/blog/f/team-trust-assessment.

Toggenburg, Christoph von. "This Is What Makes a Good Leader—and a Better Team." World Economic Forum, February 27, 2020. https://www.weforum.org/agenda/2020/02/leadership-lessons-how-to-build-dynamic-teams/.

Tuckman, Bruce W. "Leadership Teams: Developing and Sustaining High Performance." *Management Decision* 48, no. 2 (January 1, 2010): 340–44. https://doi.org/10.1108/00251741011022653.

Varela, Otmar, and Esther Mead. "Teamwork Skill Assessment: Development of a Measure for Academia." *Journal of Education for Business* 93, no. 4 (2018): 172–82. https://doi.org/10.1080/08832323.2018.1433124.

Chapter 8: Improving Organizational Results

AIHR. "About Us: We Are AIHR." Accessed June 19, 2020. https://www.aihr.com/about-us/.

Bhatti, M Ishaq, H M Awan, and Z Razaq. "The Key Performance Indicators (KPIs) and Their Impact on Overall Organizational Performance." *Qual. Quant.* 48 (2014): 3127–43.

BMI. "Business Model Canvas." Accessed May 7, 2020. https://www.businessmodelsinc.com/about-bmi/tools/business-model-canvas/.

Doerr, John, and Kris Duggan. *Measure What Matters: How Bono, the Gates Foundation, and Google Rock the World with OKRs.* New York: Penguin, 2017.

Doran, George T. "There's a SMART Way to Write Management's Goals and Objectives." *Manage. Rev.* 70, no. 11 (1981): 35–36.

Eccles, Robert G. "The Performance Measurement Manifesto." *Harvard Business Review* 69, no. 1 (1991): 131–37.

Editorial Team. "OKR vs KPI—a Delineation." Workpath, September 27, 2018. https://www.workpath.com/en/magazine/okr-vs-kpi-a-delineation/.

Forsey, Caroline. "Goals vs Objectives: The Simple Breakdown." HubSpot, April 24, 2019. https://blog.hubspot.com/marketing/goals-vs-objectives.

Grove, Andrew S. *High Output Management.* New York: Knopf Doubleday Publishing Group, 2015.

Kaplan, Robert S. "Conceptual Foundations of the Balanced Scorecard." In *Handbooks of Management Accounting Research*, edited by Christopher S Chapman, Anthony G Hopwood, and Michael D Shields, 3:1253–69. Elsevier, 2009. https://doi.org/10.1016/S1751-3243(07)03003-9.

———. "Lead and Manage Your Organization with the Balanced Scorecard." *Balanced Scorecard Report*, 2002.

Kaplan, Robert S, and David P Norton. "The Balanced Scorecard—Measures That Drive Performance." *Harv. Bus. Rev.* 70, no. 1 (January 1992): 71–79.

Kenny, Graham. "Create KPIs That Reflect Your Strategic Priorities." *Harvard Business Review*, February 4, 2020. https://hbr.org/2020/02/create-kpis-that-reflect-your-strategic-priorities.

Medne, Aija, and Inga Lapina. "Sustainability and Continuous Improvement of Organization: Review of Process-Oriented Performance Indicators." *J. Open Innov. Technol. Mark. Complex* 5, no. 3 (2019): 1–14.

Niven, Paul R, and Ben Lamorte. *Objectives and Key Results: Driving Focus, Alignment, and Engagement with OKRs.* New Jersey: John Wiley & Sons, 2016.

Okfalisa, Rose Alinda Alias, Naomie Salim, and Kuan Yew Wong. "Metric for Strategy Implementation: Measuring and Monitoring the Performance." *IEEE Symp. Ind. Elec. & Appl.* 1 (2009): 29–34. https://doi.org/10.1109/ISIEA.2009.5356497.

Osterwalder, Alexander. "A Better Way to Think about Your Business Model." *Harvard Business Review*, May 6, 2013. https://hbr.org/2013/05/a-better-way-to-think-about-yo.

Osterwalder, Alexander, and Yves Pigneur. *Business Model Generation: A Handbook for Visionaries, Game Changers, and Challengers.* Hoboken, NJ: John Wiley & Sons, 2010.

Silva, Fernanda Antunes da, and Milton Borsato. "Organizational Performance and Indicators: Trends and Opportunities." *Procedia Manufacturing* 11 (January 1, 2017): 1925–32. https://doi.org/10.1016/j.promfg.2017.07.336.

"The Four Perspectives of the Balanced Scorecard." Balanced Scorecard Institute. Accessed May 7, 2020. https://balancedscorecard.org/bsc-basics/articles-videos/the-four-perspectives-of-the-balanced-scorecard/.

Vulpen, Erik van. "21 HR Data Sources for Analytics." AIHR Analytics, March 2, 2020. https://www.analyticsinhr.com/blog/hr-data-sources/.

Chapter 9: Looking Ahead

"A Global Standard for Lifelong Learning and Worker Engagement to Support Advanced Manufacturing." White Paper. World Economic Forum, October 2019. http://www3.weforum.org/docs/WEF_Guiding_principles_to_enable_production_workers_for_the_Future_of_work_in_manufacturing.pdf.

Agarwal, Dimple, Josh Bersin, Gaurav Lahiri, Jeff Schwartz, and Erica Volini. "Citizenship and Social Impact: Society Holds the Mirror." Deloitte, March 28, 2018. https://www2.deloitte.com/us/en/insights/focus/human-capital-trends/2018/corporate-citizenship-social-impact.html.

Amesheva, Inna. "Five Technology Trends Defining the Future of Corporate Sustainability." *Eco-business*, August 28, 2017. https://www.eco-business.com/opinion/five-technology-trends-defining-the-future-of-corporate-sustainability/.

Bersin, Josh. "HR Technology 2020: Disruption Ahead." *Josh Bersin*, August 30, 2019. https://joshbersin.com/2019/08/hr-technology-2020-disruption-ahead/.

Burton, Joan. *WHO Healthy Workplace Framework and Model: Background and Supporting Literature and Practices.* Geneva: World Health Organization, 2010. https://apps.who.int/iris/bitstream/handle/10665 /113144/9789241500241_eng.pdf.

Carr, Evan W, Andrew Reece, Gabriella Rosen Kellerman, and Alexi Robichaux. "The Value of Belonging at Work." *Harvard Business Review*, December 16, 2019. https://hbr.org/2019/12/the-value-of-belonging-at-work.

Connecting Credentials. "Competency Is the New Currency." Accessed June 20, 2020. http://connectingcredentials.org/wp-content/ uploads/2018/03/Competency.pdf.

"Data-Driven Decisions: The Importance of Being Guided by Data Not Only in Times of Emergency." SDG Group, March 31, 2020. https://www. sdggroup.com/en/insights/blog/data-driven-decisions-importance-being-guided-data-not-only-times-emergency.

Eswaran, Vijay. "The Business Case for Diversity Is Now Overwhelming." World Economic Forum, April 29, 2019. https://www.weforum.org/ agenda/2019/04/business-case-for-diversity-in-the-workplace/.

Florida, Robert, and Oded Netzer. "How Leaders Can Make Sound Decisions on COVID-19 with Scarce Data to Guide Them." Impakter, April 7, 2020. https://impakter.com/how-leaders-can-make-sound-decisions-on-covid-19-with-scarce-data-to-guide-them/.

Forth, Steven. "Introducing Open Competency Models." Ibbaka, September 29, 2019. https://www.ibbaka.com/ibbaka-talent-blog/ introducing-open-competency-models.

"ILR Information & Resources." US Chamber Foundation, November 25, 2019. https://www.uschamberfoundation.org/t3-innovation-network/ ilr-pilot-program.

King, Eden, and Veronica Gilrane. "Social Science Strategies for Managing Diversity: Industrial and Organizational Opportunities to Enhance Inclusion." White Paper. Society for Industrial and Organizational Psychology, 2015. https://www.shrm.org/hr-today/ trends-and-forecasting/special-reports-and-expert-views/Documents/ SHRM-SIOP%20Diversity.pdf.

Lindecrantz, Erik, Madeleine Tjon Pian Gi, and Stefano Zerbi. "Personalizing the Customer Experience: Driving Differentiation in Retail." McKinsey, April 28, 2020. https://www.mckinsey.com/industries/retail/our-insights/personalizing-the-customer-experience-driving-differentiation-in-retail.

Moretti, Jessica M, and Don Moretti. "Recent Trends in Preemployment Assessment." White Paper. Society for Industrial and Organizational Psychology, 2018. https://www.siop.org/Portals/84/docs/White%20Papers/PreAssess.pdf.

"Open Badges: New Opportunities to Recognize and Validate Achievements Digitally." UNESCO, January 13, 2020. https://iite.unesco.org/highlights/open-badges-new-opportunities-to-recognize-and-validate-achievements-digitally/.

Osborn, Chris, and Les Wight. "AICC, SCORM, Tin Can API, XAPI: Which Standard and Why?" *Training Mag*, December 21, 2015. https://trainingmag.com/aicc-scorm-tin-can-api-xapi-which-standard-and-why/.

"Our Shared Digital Future Building an Inclusive, Trustworthy and Sustainable Digital Society." World Economic Forum, December 2018. http://www3.weforum.org/docs/WEF_Our_Shared_Digital_Future_Report_2018.pdf.

Rainie, Lee, and Janna Anderson. "The Future of Jobs and Jobs Training." Pew Research Center, May 3, 2017. http://www.pewinternet.org/2017/05/03/the-future-of-jobs-and-jobs-training/.

Renner, Dale. "Transforming The Customer Experience: Personalization." *Forbes*, November 1, 2018. https://www.forbes.com/sites/forbestechcouncil/2018/11/01/transforming-the-customer-experience-personalization/.

Schloss, Joanna. "The Art of Personalization." *CMS Wire*, August 7, 2015. https://www.cmswire.com/analytics/the-art-of-personalization/.

Shinn, Nathan. "Weighing Consumption-based Billing for Business Success?" *Forbes*, October 3, 2019. https://www.forbes.com/sites/forbesfinancecouncil/2019/10/03/weighing-consumption-based-billing-for-business-success/.

"SHRM Competency Model." SHRM, 2012. https://www.shrm.org/LearningAndCareer/competency-model/Documents/Full%20Competency%20Model%2011%202_10%201%202014.pdf.

Society for Industrial and Organizational Psychology. "Principles for the Validation and Use of Personnel Selection Procedures." Guideline. Society for Industrial and Organizational Psychology, August 2018.

Spagnoletto, Lyuba, Dianah AlabdulJabbar, and Har Jalihal. "HR4. 0: Shaping People Strategies in the Fourth Industrial Revolution." White Paper. World Economic Forum, 2019. http://www3.weforum.org/docs/WEF_NES_Whitepaper_HR4.0.pdf.

"The Future of Corporate Responsibility." Pew Research Center, July 5, 2012. https://www.pewresearch.org/internet/2012/07/05/the-future-of-corporate-responsibility/.

"The Future of Education and Skills: Education 2030." OECD, 2018. https://www.oecd.org/education/2030-project/contact/E2030_Flyer_2019.pdf.

"The Future of Workplace Learning: Training and Responsible Business Practice." *Development and Learning in Organizations: An International Journal* 21, no. 2 (January 1, 2007): 31–34. https://doi.org/10.1108/14777280710727398.

United Nations Conference on Trade and Development. "Digital Economy Report 2019: Value Creation and Capture—Implications for Developing Countries." UNCTAD, 2019. https://doi.org/10.18356/c7dc937a-en.

"White Paper on Interoperable Learning Records." White Paper. American Workforce Policy Advisory Board, September 2019. https://www.imsglobal.org/sites/default/files/articles/ILR_White_Paper_FINAL_EBOOK.pdf.

WHO. "Workplace Health Promotion." World Health Organization, December 8, 2010. https://www.who.int/occupational_health/topics/workplace/en/index1.html.

World Economic Forum Centre for the New Economy, and Society Willis Towers Watson (WTW)(Firm). "Strategies for the New Economy: Skills as the Currency of the Labour Market." World Economic Forum, January 2019. http://www3.weforum.org/docs/WEF_2019_Strategies_for_the_New_Economy_Skills.pdf.

ABOUT
THE AUTHORS

ERIC SHEPHERD has led international businesses and associations focused on talent, assessments, and success. As CEO of Questionmark, an assessment software company, Eric helped grow the organization's software and SaaS platform into a multi-million-dollar international enterprise with tens of millions of assessments delivered per year. Eric has led industry efforts and open standards initiatives to promote best practices for assessments, learning, competencies, and interoperability. As a recognized thought leader and futurist, Eric cofounded the Talent Transformation Guild as a community of professionals preparing for the new world of work. www.talenttransformation.com

JOAN PHAUP is an award-winning newspaper reporter turned human-interest columnist, technical writer, radio editorialist, and public relations executive. As public relations manager for assessment software provider Questionmark, she helped educational institutions, businesses, and government agencies appreciate the potential of computerized and online testing. Joan now provides editorial services to businesses, magazines, nonfiction authors, and nonprofit organizations in the United States, Latin America, and Europe. www.joanphaup.com

CPSIA information can be obtained
at www.ICGtesting.com
Printed in the USA
LVHW090129211020
669351LV00007B/936